D0044586

$\mathcal{A}$NGELS
IN OUR MIDST

ANGELS IN OUR MIDST

Compiled by the Editors of *Guideposts*
formerly published as *Angels Among Us*

DOUBLEDAY
New York London Toronto Sydney Auckland

PUBLISHED BY DOUBLEDAY
a division of Bantam Doubleday Dell Publishing Group, Inc.
1540 Broadway, New York, New York 10036

DOUBLEDAY and the portrayal of an anchor with a dolphin are trademarks of
Doubleday, a division of Bantam Doubleday Dell Publishing Group, Inc.

Angels in Our Midst was originally published under the title *Angels Among Us* by
Guideposts Associates, Inc. in 1993. The Doubleday edition is published by
arrangement with Guideposts Associates, Inc.

ISBN 0-385-47536-5

Printed in the United States of America

CONTENTS

IV. ANGELS AT LARGE

$\mathcal{T}$O THE READER

The Wall Street Journal for May 12, 1992, carried an article by staff reporter R. Gustav Niebuhr about people who have been helped by guardian angels and the effect that the experience has had on their lives. "After a hiatus of maybe 300 years and much skepticism," Niebuhr wrote, "angels are making a comeback."

Comeback, indeed! Angels have never been away. But in a time of increased interest in these heavenly beings, more people are coming forth to tell of their encounters with them. In the Bible there are angels to be read about from Genesis in the Old Testament to the last chapter of Revelation in the New. Now, in these pages, you can read about the angels who visit us today. They are all ministering spirits who by their presence provide not just succor but reassuring evidence of a loving God who is forever watching over us.

When you have finished reading this book, it's likely you will have a new appreciation of a phenomenon that heretofore you may have only sensed. You'll start looking back over your own life, recalling certain inexplicable happenings that left you puzzled and in awe. It is then that you will begin to understand some of the mystery and beauty of the events related in these stories. It is then that you will begin to alert your ears to what the poet Betty Banner has heard as "the swish of passing wings."

I

ANGELS UNAWARE

In No Strange Land

O world invisible, we view thee,
O world intangible, we touch thee,
O world unknowable, we know thee,
Inapprehensible, we clutch thee!

Does the fish soar to find the ocean,
The eagle plunge to find the air—
That we ask of the stars in motion
If they have rumor of thee there?

Not where the wheeling systems darken,
And our benumbed conceiving soars!—
The drift of pinions, would we hearken,
Beats at our own clay-shuttered doors.

The angels keep their ancient places;—
Turn but a stone, and start a wing!
'Tis ye, 'tis your estrangèd faces,
That miss the many-splendored thing.

But (when so sad thou canst not sadder)
Cry,—and upon thy so sore loss
Shall shine the traffic of Jacob's ladder
Pitched betwixt Heaven and Charing Cross.

Yea, in the night, my Soul, my daughter,
Cry,—clinging Heaven by the hems;
And lo, Christ walking on the water
Not of Genesareth, but Thames!

—Francis Thompson

I
⒜NGELS UNAWARE

Sometimes they come in disguise, just like in a good mystery story. You have no way of suspecting their true identity as angels of God until, their deed done, they leave and you are left scratching your head in puzzlement.

Here in "Angels Unaware" you'll find a number of unorthodox characters for your head-scratching. And your astonishment. Some of them come giving validity to the Latin (*angelus*) and the Greek (*angelos*) meanings for our word "angel"—*messenger*. They come as a tall blond man pointing at a hole in the ice through which a boy has disappeared; they come as a neatly dressed Chinese gentleman who holds four soldiers at bay; they come even in the form of a large white dog who leads the way to a discovery. They come; they disappear, never to be seen again.

It's not hard to see why everyone loves a good mystery. And why not? Life itself is mysterious, a matter of awe. Faith in God is a mystery, a matter of wonder and reverence and of trust in things unseen.

And who can say that these mysterious strangers are not the chosen messengers of God?

THE TALL BLOND STRANGER

Nelson Sousa

On December 19, 1979, my partner Ray and I were working as construction divers at a bridge site near Somers Point, New Jersey. Snow had begun to fall early, and by noon it had gotten so heavy we had to knock off work.

As we waded through parking-lot drifts, I noticed that my boss's car didn't have snow tires.

"Hey John," I said to him, "why don't you let me drive you home? I don't think you'll make it with those tires."

John considered for a moment, then nodded. "Okay, Nelson, you might be right." But as he started toward my pickup, he stopped and turned back to his car. "Oh, I almost forgot," he said, reaching into his trunk. "Here's your spare dry suit I borrowed last month. I finally remembered to bring it back."

I was about to take the suit to our on-site trailer office where we store gear. But since it had some holes in it, I decided to take it home to repair. I threw it into the back of my pickup. It was the first time in my ten years of diving that I had traveled anywhere with one of these protective rubber suits. They were always stored at work.

The drive north through the snow was rough; stop-and-go all the way. What should have taken us one hour took over three. But we spent the time talking about Christmas and the toys we were buying our kids.

I didn't really mind going out of the way for John, but by the time we got to his turnoff it was past three o'clock. We turned into his street. A fire engine roared by and stopped at the end of the block. There was a big commotion down there.

"O dear God, no . . ." John said. Ahead was an alarming tableau: a frozen pond, an ominous black hole in its center. Fire trucks with lights flashing and people crowding the bank. A woman squalling and weeping.

"Somebody must have fallen through the ice," Ray said.

I pulled the pickup over to the side, jumped out, grabbed my dry suit from the back, pulled it on and ran to the pond. Ray stumbled along behind me zipping me up.

A grim-faced firefighter told us that a six-year-old boy had walked out on the ice and fallen in. "But it's hopeless," he groaned, "the ice is too thin for us to get out there." Two men had already tried. Even a ladder laid on the ice didn't work. And the water was so cold that anyone falling into it would be shocked into unconsciousness in minutes.

"_I'll try,_" I said. Someone tied a rope around my waist and I headed out, splintering the ice into shards as I beat my way through it. By the time I reached the hole where the boy had disappeared, my hands were bleeding from the exertion.

Icy water surged through the holes in the suit I was going to repair. I knew I had only a minute or two for a dive. Then I discovered I had left my heavy diver's belt back at the job. Without it to weight me down, it would be hard to swim underwater in my buoyant rubber suit. But I _had_ to get down to the bottom.

All I could do was force my body down. The water looked black. About six feet down I touched bottom, then bobbed up like a cork. Up and down, up and down I plunged, working partway around the opening in the ice frantically feeling for a body. But there was nothing, only frigid water and a slick muddy bottom. _Where was he?_

Gasping, coughing from exhaustion, I cried out in desperation: "He's not here! I can't find him. Where is he?"

Looking up across the pond, I saw a tall blond man in a light jacket standing by himself in the snow. He raised his arm and pointed to a spot on the side of the hole opposite me.

I pushed to the spot and thrust myself down. The ice-cold water closed over my head, and then my foot touched something. The boy's body! I surged up again. Now, with violent arm movements, I

forced myself down and wrapped my feet around the body and drew it up. Floating on my back, I pulled the limp, sodden form across my chest and held him tight.

The little boy's soaked blue jacket seemed glued to him. I pulled back the hood covering his head and screamed. The pinched face was as blue as the jacket. He was not breathing. I could not look at him anymore.

"Pull me back!" I yelled, and the rope tightened around me as firefighters heaved on it, hauling me to the bank. John jumped into the water, took the form and passed it to waiting medics. I staggered upright, untied the rope and headed toward them when two policemen grabbed me. "C'mon," one urged, "get into our squad car and warm up."

"But the boy! . . ." I yelled. By now the ambulance's doors had slammed shut and it sped away, siren wailing. I stood shaking my head, feeling helpless, wishing I could have saved him.

John, my boss, took me to his house where I warmed up some more and then Ray and I drove home. When I walked in, my wife, Patricia, was preparing dinner. I didn't even kiss her, just stumbled over to the sofa and slumped down sobbing. It had all been so useless.

Pat looked at Ray. "Nelson pulled a little boy out of the pond," Ray explained.

Patricia had cooked my favorite dish, beef stroganoff, but I couldn't touch it. I could only sit on the living-room sofa thinking about the poor little fellow and how his parents were feeling.

Patricia called the hospital where the boy had been taken. They told her that little Michael Polukard had been under water for around ten minutes. He was unconscious, in serious condition; a priest had given him last rites; but he was alive.

What a Christmas! I thought, staring into the glowing lights on our tree. Under it was our Nativity scene; the manger bed was empty—our custom is to place the Baby Jesus in it on Christmas Eve. I felt even worse thinking about a real little bed that was empty that night.

I looked gloomily around the room. On the TV set stood two white angels Patricia had made for the house that year. One held a string of stars, the other played a harp. How frivolous it all seemed now. Angels! I remembered how my Portuguese grandmother used to tell us kids about the angels who sang of Jesus' birth to the shepherds that long-ago night. But that night angels and Jesus didn't seem very real to me. And yet, my heart grieved so for the little boy that I did the only thing left for me to do. I leaned my head down and prayed for him. I asked God to help him live.

Hours passed as I sat, moodily staring at the wall. Patricia put our two little girls to bed and Ray tried to encourage me. "He's still alive, you know," Ray said. "There's hope. You should just be grateful that you knew where to find him in that pond."

I looked up. "I didn't know where he was, Ray," I said. "It was that big blond guy who pointed me to the right spot. If it hadn't been for him, I never would have found the boy."

Ray looked puzzled. "That's the strangest thing, Nelson. You keep talking about some guy on the other side of the pond but" . . . he scratched his head . . . "there wasn't anybody over there."

About nine o'clock the phone rang. Patricia took it, then handed it to me. "It's Michael's father, he wants to thank you."

With shaking hand, I took the phone. "Don't worry about me," I blurted, "all I want to know is how your little boy is."

Stan Polukard said Michael was still in serious condition, but it looked as though he was going to make it. The very coldness of the water had slowed Michael's body functions, he explained, reducing his need for oxygen. I gave a big sigh of relief and, in my heart, thanked God for saving the little boy. Then I was able to fall into bed and sleep.

We kept in close touch with the hospital the following days, but the news wasn't good. The Polukards had been warned that Michael might have extensive brain damage. The doctors worried about all the time that had passed before his heart and lungs had resumed functioning. A test of his brain by an electroencephalogram had shown "inconclusive" results. Doctors said that only after he regained consciousness would they know how much he'd been damaged.

We learned that his mother and father moved into the hospital to stay with the boy. The news reported that they were praying for him around the clock. People everywhere sent encouraging messages, saying they were praying with them. I didn't know that there were that many strong believers.

The papers kept up a running account of Michael's plight. Eileen and Stan Polukard continued to talk to their little boy, who lay unconscious, connected to a respirator, a heart monitor and intravenous lines. The doctors tried to protect them from false hope.

"Remember," one doctor warned Eileen, "the child you knew may no longer exist."

On the third day, Friday, the medical staff took Michael off the respirator. Stan and Eileen continued their patient, prayerful vigil at their son's bedside. Then, opening his eyes, he slowly turned toward them. "Hi Mom, hi Dad," he whispered.

On Monday afternoon, Christmas Eve, we got a phone call.

"Michael's home!" my wife shouted. The Polukards had called saying that tests showed Michael completely well and normal and that they could take him home. They invited us to their house to celebrate with them.

Patricia and I bundled our two little girls into the car and hurried over.

Michael was dressed in pajamas and sitting on the living-room sofa when we came in. "Do you know who I am?" I asked. For the rest of the evening he wouldn't leave my side. And as we talked he happened to mention that one of the first things he saw when he opened his eyes in the hospital was an angel.

"An angel?" I said, surprised.

There had been an angel there, all right. A big paper angel had hung over Michael's bed as part of the hospital's Christmas decorations.

Angels again. Once more I thought of that mysterious time my grandmother used to tell us about, when the angels spoke to the shepherds in the fields and told them about the little Baby lying in a manger.

I pictured our own little crèche in our living room at home. When we'd get back, our two little girls would place the Baby Jesus in His manger bed.

    I glanced up and saw Michael in his father's arms and I gave thanks to the One Who had sent us His Son . . . and Who, I now knew for certain, sent His help, somehow, someway, so that another little bed would be warm tonight.

    But there was another picture in my mind, a tall blond man standing alone in the snow, beside the pond, pointing. Who was he? In all the weeks and months to come, I would find no one who had seen him there. On this happy Christmas Eve, in a room filled with quiet celebration, I couldn't help but wonder.

*T*HE LIGHT IN THE COURTROOM

Richard S. Whaley

When I was a young man and had practiced law in the State of
South Carolina only a short time, I was surprised one morning by a
visit from an uncle of mine. He was one of the few remaining
Southerners of the old school; courtesy and punctiliousness were
the keynotes of his every act.

"Dick," he drawled, "many years ago, your grandfather on your
mother's side had a family of slaves, by the name of Holmes. Some
of the Holmes boys now seem to be tied up with a bunch of bad
characters. There's been a murder down in the County, and the
prosecutor is pressing a case against the Holmeses. It will be coming up for a trial in the next session. That Holmes family was
mighty good to us Whaleys in the days of our troubles. I been kind
of hoping that there is some mistake somewhere. But I know nothing about it. Somehow, I can't just stand by, and I kind of reckoned
that you, knowing the law, might take over."

I confess that in those days I was looking for better retainers. In
similar cases, about all I received as a fee would be perhaps a dozen
chickens or so. I was just about to find some good excuse when
Uncle Ben, whose piercing eyes seemed to read my thoughts,
spoke aloud to himself as if I was not present at all.

"Yes, when those Yanks cleaned us out," Uncle murmured, "the
food situation become desperate. The Holmes family, down to the
smallest curly head, foraged all day long, and late into the evening.

"We were about to give up after days without nourishment, with grandma and grandpa very feeble. The Holmeses returned, built up the kitchen fire, and soon prepared the best-tasting soup and meals we had for a long, long time. I have often heard it said that the lives of the old folks were saved by that soup. Those former slaves kept us alive—and well. They provided for us a long time, till things got better."

I felt ashamed of any selfishness. All I could do was to stammer, boylike, "Then, if it hadn't been for the Holmeses, I might not be here, much less be a lawyer."

As if satisfied with my reaction, my Uncle Ben stood up and with a most courteous bow, shook my hand without further word and left me to come to my own decision.

I was soon doing nothing else but investigating all the facts of the murder case and the incidents in the lives of the Holmes boys. I also got to know almost every twig in the neighborhood of the crime. I watched the mannerisms of the suspected boys, but while I felt convinced of their innocence, I could find no way to prove it. There were simply too many circumstances that, unexplained, pointed to their guilt. The very simple-mindedness of the boys, which convinced me of their honesty, was a weakness against them. When the trial started I was sick at heart over my lack of a good case.

Day after day, the prosecutor fitted in his condemning evidence like pieces of mosaic. Then, like the keystone of an arch, he produced as his main witness a detective who had a natural clarity of expression and a highly impressive delivery. Word after word beat into the minds of the jury, who seemed almost hypnotized.

Late one afternoon when the prosecutor was about to conclude his case, the court ordered an adjournment to the next day. When the courtroom emptied, I sank down in my chair exhausted, beaten. I seemed to breathe rather than speak. "O God, do not allow an injustice to happen to these boys. Let Your Holy Spirit pour wisdom and strength through me. We are lost without Your help."

I sat a long while lost in a sense of prayer—of growing assurance of God's mercy and justice. I was roused by the sound of footsteps in the big empty chamber and looked up.

There stood a complete stranger. He approached me and said, "Did you know, son, a man can get a detective certificate and badge for two dollars? See, here is the Savannah newspaper advertisement where it says so."

"Well, what of it?" I muttered wearily. The stranger handed me the paper, gave an odd smile and nod, and sauntered off again without an answer. I stared at the printed words and my mind began to click. I began to pace around the room in mounting excitement. *Was prayer answered that quickly?*

For a scene had flashed through my mind—a scene that had occurred several days ago in the corridor. It was such an insignificant incident that it seemed amazing that I remembered it at all. A certain man had approached the prosecutor's star witness, the detective, and said in a rather ribald manner: "Jim, when are you going to pay me that two bucks you borrowed?"

The next day in court this detective was in the witness stand when the judge tersely announced to me: "Your cross-examination." His manner plainly indicated that he figured I had a hopeless case.

I stood up with a prayer—and the Savannah newspaper in my hand. Then to everyone's amazement I asked the detective, "Did you borrow two dollars a while back from Mr. Jones? I heard him ask you the other day when you were going to pay."

The detective was caught off guard. He reddened and stammered. The prosecutor leaped to his feet and objected. The jury stared at me with looks of both pity and bafflement.

"Of course, in so important a case as this, you are prepared to submit your certificate entitling you to act as a detective," I insisted calmly.

There was no mistaking the red-faced look on the detective's face now as he handed forth his certificate. One glance at the fancy engraved paper and its recent date was enough for me. Suddenly it seemed as if all the power in the universe was in my sinews. I produced the *Savannah Journal*, read the ad to the judge and jury, and took this fling at the thoroughly abashed detective who had tried to pass as an expert:

"And with the two dollars you borrowed from Jones, you bought this certificate and badge!"

The detective was completely discredited when he admitted it. Nothing he said thereafter had any effect on the jury. In fact, his impressive delivery was gone and he was in a hurry to get it all over with and leave all those disgusted and mocking faces in the courtroom.

The jury remained out but a few moments. Their verdict: "Not guilty." The Holmes boys were free.

"Illuminate me with thy Holy Spirit," said Dr. Samuel Johnson. Whenever I read this prayer I cannot help but think of that trial which was so significant in my life, not only because it paid off a family debt of saving life for life; not only because it kept two innocent men from a shameful end; and not only because it chalked up justice to blacks in the South—but because early in my career it taught me to seek God's help and ask for His Holy Spirit to enlighten me.

All my life I've begun my day in court with a silent, earnest prayer. I would not dream of undertaking work without it.

*T*HE FIRE STORM

Joe Stevenson

It was hot when I got back from church—August-Sunday-morning hot. Thunderstorms growled and lightning flickered over the twenty-five thousand acres of untouched rangeland behind our house, which sits back some two hundred yards from the Mount Rose Highway near Reno, Nevada.

I'd had a busy morning. First I'd helped my wife Janice load the car for a trip to Las Vegas where she planned to visit her sister for a week. She was taking the children with her. This meant that I would be alone with our dog B.J. and our two cats. I was sorry to see the family leave, but I was kind of looking forward to a week of peaceful bachelorhood. Every husband knows the feeling.

After they were gone, I drove down the dirt road to the highway and on to the Mount Rose Evangelical Free Church where I taught a discussion group. The topic that morning, I remember, was 1 Corinthians.

I also remember the feeling of satisfaction I had when I came back and saw our house sitting there in a sea of sagebrush and mesquite, silhouetted against the blue Nevada sky. It had taken us ten years of planning and two of building to get that house, and we all loved it. We considered it the last home we'd live in.

At about 2:30 that afternoon, lightning started a brush fire about two miles from our house. I was concerned—any fire in August is extremely dangerous because the vegetation is so dry—but the wind was blowing out of the southwest, which meant that the fire would be moving away from us. My neighbor, Tony Brayton, came over to watch it with me. We both felt sure it would be contained before it could possibly reach us.

Still, just as a precaution, I loaded a few belongings into the car. Then I got out a hose and began wetting down our roof and the brand-new deck I had just added to the house. Other people in the area were watching the fire, too. Three times the phone rang with people calling to say that they were praying we would be all right. There was comfort and reassurance in that.

But abruptly, at about 4:45, the wind swung around 180 degrees. The southwester suddenly became a northeaster. The flames were heading straight for us.

Tony, who had left about ten minutes earlier, came racing back. We stood there, half-paralyzed by what we saw. What had been a small brush fire was now a gigantic fire storm roaring toward us, consuming everything before it in a wall of flame fifteen to thirty feet high and half a mile wide. On it came at an incredible pace, sucking oxygen from the air at ground-level in front of it and creating tornados of fire that shot fifty feet into the smoke-blackened sky. The crackling sounds it made were terrifying. It was as if some gigantic demon bent on our destruction had materialized from nowhere. It roared up the hillside, leaping across a canyon sixty feet deep and a hundred feet wide as if the canyon weren't there. Its speed was incredible. In seconds it would be upon us.

I snatched open the door and screamed for B.J., but there was no sign of her and no time to look for her. Tony and I dropped the hoses and ran for our lives. As we ran, I said the fastest wide-awake running prayer I ever said in all my forty-two years of living. I said, "Lord, I put my house and everything in it into Your hands." And then, remembering what St. Paul said about the importance of giving thanks for everything, good or bad, I managed to pray

(although I didn't feel like it at all), "Lord, no matter what happens, I thank You for it and praise You."

I jumped into my little Omni. Tony flung himself into my other car. We tore down the road to Tony's house, picked up his wife, warned a family in a third house, and raced for the highway. Behind us, the fiery monster swept on, roaring, hissing, crackling, engulfing everything.

At the highway, I stepped out of my car and stared back at a wall of flame and smoke. How do you react when everything you've spent twelve years dreaming of and working for is destroyed in ten seconds of searing flame? Do you swear? Do you scream? Do you cry? Others were doing all those things, but I didn't, because the thought that was uppermost in my mind at that moment was: *You're a Christian, Joe, so act like one. Remember: "All things work together for good to those who love God." Praise God.* So I did praise Him, out loud, although I know some people thought I was crazy, or in shock, or both.

We stayed at the highway another ten minutes or so, watching other houses become engulfed, too dazed to do or say anything. Then the flames were on us at the highway, and police told us we had to move farther up the mountain. Later I heard that 125 utility poles burned along the highway that day.

At this point something happened that was very strange, although it didn't seem strange at the time. As I walked toward my car, a young man with dark hair, dressed in a T-shirt and blue jeans, called to me. "Hey, you in the white shirt." I didn't know the young man, and actually I was wearing a light-yellow shirt, but I pointed to myself questioningly. He looked directly at me and said. "I got on your roof and watered it down for you." Tony also heard him say this.

I was sure he had mistaken me for someone else, since no one could possibly have gone near my house after I had left. I thanked him anyway, and thought no more about it.

Later, at a friend's house in Lake Tahoe, I was able to reach Janice at her sister's. Having to tell her that our dream house had burned to the ground was harder than watching the fire. All she said was, "Thank God you're all right."

The threat of fire along the roads made it impossible to get back to Reno that night. I called the fire department repeatedly, but could get no information. At one point I called a church couple, Chauncey and Betty Fairchild, who I knew could see my house from across the valley. "Joe," Chauncey said, "we watched the whole thing through our binoculars. When we saw the flames change direction and head for you, our entire family formed a prayer circle and prayed for your safety and the safety of your home. And, Joe, it's still standing."

I thanked him, but I didn't believe him. Maybe, I thought, he could still see the shell of my house, but I knew nothing could have survived the fire storm. My house was surrounded by dry brush and wood that my wife had asked me repeatedly to clear away.

When I got back to the house soon after dawn the next morning, I couldn't believe my eyes. This is what I found:

The fire had burned to within ten feet of the house, and all around it, *but no farther*. House and contents were untouched.

The power line coming into my house had melted, thirty feet in the air, and had fallen to the ground thirty feet from the house.

The telephone lines above the power lines had fused.

My chicken coop, just forty feet from the house, was scorched and smoldering . . . but all ten chickens were alive.

The dog and two cats were unharmed. The cats were outside, one in the garage and one on the back steps. The dog was inside, very glad to see me.

My bridge, which is two hundred yards from the house and not even on my property, was untouched, while my neighbor's bridge just fifteen feet away, was completely destroyed. Only dry brush was between them.

Of the seven houses in my area, three were completely destroyed. All the others were damaged, two seriously.

How do I account for all this? How do I explain the fact that absolutely nothing I owned was touched by the fire, whether it was on my property or not? All I can do is tell you what I think.

I've been a Christian almost all my life, but I know that my faith isn't as strong as it might be. And this may be true of a lot of church-going people; we know we're Christians and we think that's good enough. But I believe there are times when God wants to test our faith—and reinforce it. I also believe—although I can't pretend to understand it fully—that sometimes when we are able to thank God in the face of seeming disaster, and place ourselves unreservedly in His hands, and get out of His way, He can and will do astounding things for us.

The intensity of that fire on that morning of August 9, 1981, cannot be exaggerated. At the time I was working for the Nevada Bell System, and so I know something about cables. It would have taken at least 1800 degrees of heat to melt those power lines that were thirty feet above the ground. Maybe 2000 degrees. And yet my house, thirty feet away, wasn't even *marked*. To me, that was God speaking clearly to me, and He was saying, "I'm here, I'm real, I care." He did reinforce my faith, because He knew it needed reinforcing. I'll never be quite so smug or so casual about it again.

Then there's the enigma of the young man, whom I've never seen again. How did he know who I was? How did he know it was my house? When I finally got back to the house, the hose I had dropped on the deck was now on the roof. At least three witnesses have told me that they saw somebody on the roof. But Tony and I left by the only route that was not in flames. How could anyone get there without our seeing him? And if someone did get there, how did he get up on the roof? There is no ladder. You can't just climb up because of the overhang. And, since my power line must have been the first thing to be destroyed, how could water flow through a hose from a well pumped by electricity?

I can't answer these questions. But maybe—just maybe—there's an answer in the Bible. Turn to Hebrews 13 and read the second verse. For the word "entertained," substitute the phrase "been rescued by." Then you may have a clue as to what really happened that August day on the Mount Rose Highway.

For me, it's more than a clue. I think it's the truth.

$\mathcal{G}$OD'S SECRET AGENTS

Billy Graham

Angels, whether noticed by men or not, are active in our twentieth-century world. Are we aware of them?

It was a tragic night in a Chinese city. Bandits had surrounded the mission compound sheltering hundreds of women and children. On the previous night the missionary, Miss Monsen, had been put to bed with a bad attack of malaria, and now the tempter harassed her with questions: "What will you do when the looters come here? When firing begins on this compound, what about those promises you have been trusting?" In his book, *1,000 New Illustrations* (Zondervan, 1960), Al Bryant records the result. Miss Monsen prayed, "Lord, I have been teaching these young people all these years that thy promises are true, and if they fail now, my mouth shall be forever closed; I must go home."

Throughout the next night she was up, ministering to frightened refugees, encouraging them to pray and to trust God to deliver them. Though fearful things happened all around, the bandits left the mission compound untouched.

In the morning, people from three different neighborhood families asked Miss Monsen, "Who were those four people, three sitting and one standing, quietly watching from the top of your house all night long?" When she told them that no one had been on the housetop, they refused to believe her, saying, "We saw them with our own eyes!" She then told them that God still sent angels to guard his children in their hour of danger.

We have also noted the provision of angels. On occasion they have even given food, as we know from the life of Elijah, following his triumph over the priests of Baal. Fearful, tired and discouraged, "As he lay and slept under a juniper tree, behold, then an angel touched him, and said . . . Arise and eat" (1 Kings 19:5–7). God has promised, "Are they not all ministering spirits, sent forth to minister for them who shall be heirs of salvation?" (Hebrews 1:14.)

Need we think this provisioning by angels ceased thousands of years ago?

When I was visiting the American troops during the Korean War, I was told of a small group of American marines in the First Division who had been trapped up north. With the thermometer at twenty degrees below zero, they were close to freezing to death. And they had had nothing to eat for six days. Surrender to the Chinese seemed their only hope of survival. But one of the men, a Christian, pointed out certain verses of Scripture, and taught his comrades to sing a song of praise to God. Following this they heard a crashing noise, and turned to see a wild boar rushing toward them. As they tried to jump out of his way, he suddenly stopped in his tracks. One of the soldiers raised his rifle to shoot, but before he could fire, the boar inexplicably toppled over. They rushed up to kill him only to find that he was already dead. That night they feasted on meat, and began to regain their strength.

The next morning just as the sun was rising they heard another noise. Their fear that a Chinese patrol had discovered them suddenly vanished as they found themselves face to face with a South Korean who could speak English. He said, "I will show you out." He led them through the forest and mountains to safety behind their own lines. When they looked up to thank him, they found he had disappeared.

* * *

David says of angels, "He who dwelleth in the secret place of the Most High shall abide under the shadow of the Almighty. . . . For he shall give his angels charge over thee, to keep thee in all thy ways. They shall bear thee up . . . lest thou dash thy foot against a stone" (Psalm 91:1, 11, 12).

My wife, Ruth, tells of a strange incident in a Christian bookroom in Shanghai, China. She learned of it through her father, Dr. L. Nelson Bell, who served in the hospital in Tsingkiangpu, Kiangsu province. It was at this store that Dr. Bell bought his gospel portions and tracts to distribute among his patients.

The incident occurred in 1942, after the Japanese had taken over Shanghai. One morning around nine o'clock, a Japanese truck stopped outside the bookroom. It was carrying five marines and was half-filled with books. The Christian Chinese shop assistant, who was alone at the time, realized with dismay that they had come to seize the stock. By nature timid, he felt this was more than he could endure.

Jumping from the truck, the marines made for the shop door; but before they could enter, a neatly dressed Chinese gentleman entered the shop ahead of them. Though the shop assistant knew practically all the Chinese customers who traded there, this man was a complete stranger. For some unknown reason the soldiers seemed unable to follow him, and loitered about, looking in at the four large windows, but not entering. For two hours they stood around, until after eleven, but never set foot inside the door. The stranger asked what the men wanted, and the Chinese shop assistant explained that the Japanese were seizing stocks from many of the bookshops in the city, and now this store's turn had come. The two prayed together, the stranger encouraging him, and so the two hours passed. At last the soldiers climbed into their army truck and drove away. The stranger also left, without making a single purchase or even inquiring about any items in the shop.

Later that day the shop owner, Mr. Christopher Willis (whose Chinese name was Lee) returned. The shop assistant said to him, "Mr. Lee, do you believe in angels?"

"I do," said Mr. Willis.

"So do I, Mr. Lee." Could the stranger have been one of God's protecting angels? Dr. Bell always thought so.

*W*HO MOVED THE CHAIR?

Barry Rudesill

"The Lord sustains him on his sickbed..." (Psalm 41:3, RSV)

I was suffering one of my worst asthma attacks. It was so bad that Mom took me to the hospital, where a doctor gave me a shot. "This is about the best we can do for you," he said. "If you're having problems in the morning, come back immediately."

That night I asked my parents to set up a bed for me on the living room couch. I didn't want to keep my brother up; I was wheezing and gasping for breath.

For a long while I tossed and turned. I didn't have the strength to get out of bed, so I lay there, listening to the sounds of the night, praying for relief. At last a time came when my breathing eased and I drifted off to sleep.

When I woke up, Mom was leaning over me, smiling. "Barry, how do you feel?"

"Fine," I said, breathing deeply. "No problem." Then I noticed a chair that had been pulled close to the couch as if someone had been sitting there. "Did you or Dad come in after I went to sleep?" I asked.

"No," Mom said, "we listened, but you seemed to be better."

"But when did you move the chair next to me?"

"Why, Barry," she said, "we didn't."

"I didn't, either!" I exclaimed. "I couldn't have moved last night if I had tried."

And then I remembered the feeling I'd had as I dozed off. Someone—yes, Someone—was sitting at my side.

THE WHITE DOG

Neva Joyce Coil

I pulled my car into the driveway, turned off the ignition, and opened the car door, bracing myself against the icy blast of wind and rain. As I hurried toward the house, I glanced toward the doghouse, realizing that Skipper hadn't barked when my car pulled up. I looked again. Skipper wasn't there! My heart sank as I went closer to take another look. Not only was he gone but he was dragging his chain along with him. *Why today of all days, I grumbled to myself, the coldest day of the year? If his chain gets tangled in the brush and he can't get free, he'll freeze to death out there before morning.*

Skipper was our German keeshund who had gone blind at a very early age as a result of being sprayed with a chemical substance while chasing a biker. In spite of his blindness, he was a wonderful companion, a very beautiful and smart animal, and an excellent watch dog. He guarded our home with a passion, always seeming to know when footsteps were not those of family or friends. And we could always tell whether his bark was a friendly greeting or an ominous warning of a stranger's approach. I couldn't leave such a wonderful friend out on a day like this.

We live near Toronto, in eastern Ohio, on four acres of beautiful woods. My husband and I both love it here where, with each change of season, God practices all of His artistic abilities on the woods around us. But the winters can be harsh.

I went into the house and began the task of hunting out warmer clothing. Then I phoned my daughter, Linda, who lived in town, to let her know that I was going out into the woods. Linda insisted on coming with me. While I waited for her to arrive, I wrote a note to my husband telling him what had happened and which direction we were planning to go. We always made it a practice never to go into the woods without letting someone know where we were.

Dressed warmly Linda and I headed out into the icy rain and the woods directly behind the house. Now we could hear Skipper barking, the sound echoing down through the hollows. He sounded very close. But we knew only too well that such sounds bounce off the hillsides, and though they may actually be coming from due south, you might hear the echo coming from due north. No, we could not depend on the sounds to guide us. In the not yet frozen ground we watched for other signs. We found deer tracks and many other animal tracks, but none large enough to match the paws of our large dog. Nothing to signify that Skipper had ever been there. We stayed in the woods until our coats were covered with ice. Then we trudged up over the hill and back into the house to warm ourselves and change into dry clothing for the next trip.

This time, we took the east side of the woods. Nothing. The third time, we took the west side. Every time, we prayed both aloud and silently, "Lord, please help us to find him." As the cold penetrated our bones, we became more and more discouraged, but we both knew that to quit meant Skipper would be frozen to death by morning. So we kept trudging on. The sounds of his barking spurred us on to try just one more time. Darkness was closing in on us and the rain was turning to sleet, as we headed out again.

We could still hear Skipper barking. He was beginning to sound hoarse now, and we were desperately praying, "God, please help us to find him before dark."

At the edge of the woods we stopped briefly to determine which way to go. Suddenly we were met by a very large dog I had never seen before. He was a beautiful animal, very much like a German police dog, but pure white. The dog came toward us, then stopped and stood there wagging his tail. We stood looking at him and trying to decide what to do. While we watched, he ran a little way into the woods, then returned to the same spot in front of us. A second time he ran into the woods and came back. After the third time, Linda said, "He's acting just like Lassie does in the television show when she wants someone to follow her."

So, very cautiously, we followed as he ran ahead of us and then came back to make sure that we were still behind him. Little by little Skipper's bark sounded closer and closer until we rounded a clump of bushes and there he stood right in front of us. His long fur coat was covered with ice and his chain was tangled about a clump of brush and also around an electrical tower. As we ran toward Skipper, the big white dog moved back, as though to say to us, "Come on, I won't bother you." We tried to keep an eye on him while we worked feverishly to untangle Skipper's chain, but then we completely forgot about him. When we finally had Skipper free, we looked around for the big white dog; he was nowhere to be found. He had gone out of our lives as mysteriously as he had come.

Skipper lived for another five years. Then one morning in the late fall, after the beautiful colored leaves had turned brown and fallen from the trees, I looked out the window and Skipper was gone again. The chain was there at the dog house and his collar was lying on the ground, just as though it had been unfastened. Once more Linda and I searched the woods around the house, walking through leaves that were almost the color of his beautiful long furry coat. In my heart I knew that this time we would not find him. There was no sound of his bark in the distance, only the echo of our own voices floating back to us as we called his name. Wiping away our tears, we talked about the day that the white dog had come and led us to Skipper.

And still we often ask ourselves, "Was it a dog, or was it an angel who caused our eyes to see him as a dog, because we wouldn't have followed a stranger into the woods?" We will never know the answer to that question. All we know is, that we had never seen that white dog before, we have never seen him since, but he came as an answer to prayer.

*M*EETING ANGELS UNAWARE

On life's busy thoroughfare,
We meet with angels unaware,
But we are too busy to see or hear,
Too busy to sense that God is near,
Too busy to stop and recognize
The grief that lies in another's eyes,
Too busy to offer to help or share,
Too busy to sympathize or care,
Too busy to do the good things we should,
Telling ourselves we would if we could.
But life is too swift and the pace is too great
And we dare not pause for we might be late
For our next appointment which means so much,
We are willing to brush off the Saviour's touch,
And we tell ourselves there will come a day,
We will have more time to pause on our way,
But before we know it life's sun has set,
And we've passed the Saviour, but never met,
For hurrying along life's thoroughfare,
We passed Him by and remained unaware
That within the very sight of our eye,
Unnoticed, the Son of God passed by.

—Helen Steiner Rice

II
ANGELS ON GUARD

God Hath Sent His Angel

"God hath sent his angel." Let us cry
The words aloud when any storm abates,
Or when some threatened danger passes by,
Or pain be lifted, for the one who waits
Upon the Lord will find at last the white
Releasing Presence standing close, will see
An angel bent above him in the night
To strike his chains away and set him free.

God will send his angel. Heart, this hour
May seem like some dark dungeon of despair,
But locks and bars are useless when the power
Of angel hands is working for you there.
Look up and out beyond your prison bars—
There is a stir of wings among the stars!

—Grace Noll Crowell

II

ℐNGELS ON GUARD

" 'Dennis,' Doug called softly, his voice relaxed, 'Dennis, there's an *angel* here. I can see him plain as anything. He's bright. He's trying to help us.' "

Dennis Farah was nine the year he and his little brother Douglas were trapped in a cave-in of dirt. They would have been smothered to death had it not been for the angel who was there with them, close.

That is the way with guardian angels—they stay close, waiting for the moment when they are most needed. Dennis and Doug saw their angel, and that was important because seeing the angel was the thing that took away their fear. Sometimes, as you'll find in the stories that follow, guardian angels reveal themselves by voice and other times by a quick push, a grab, a clasp of hand. And when you read the story of Traci Jacobsen's more than eighty-foot fall from a jagged cliff, you'll meet a teenager who has reason to take literal comfort in Psalm 91:11–12: "For he shall give his angels charge over thee, to keep thee in all thy ways. They shall bear thee up in their hands."

This is a passage in which you too can take comfort. That and the knowledge that a guardian angel is on your shoulder now, this very moment, watching.

THE HAND ON MY SHOULDER

Jerry Bond

Late one March evening in 1974, I was awakened by the sound of distant cries and shouts. At first I thought it was a domestic quarrel, but an urgency in the voices caused me to think it might be something more serious. I got up and opened the window. The smell of smoke, heavy and pungent, drifted into the room. And the voices, shrill with panic, cut clearly through the cool night air.

"Help me! Help me! My little girl is in there!"

Alarmed, I pulled on my pants, grabbed a flashlight, and followed the cries to Medlin Street, a block and a half away. There the house of a family named Green, a one-story brick structure, was ablaze. Black smoke was pouring out of the windows. A small crowd had gathered, mostly neighbors and a few policemen. The fire department hadn't arrived yet.

In the flickering orange-black darkness, I watched in horror as a team of men worked to pull Mr. Green, severely burned and in a state of shock, through a small window near the back of the house. Then I saw Mrs. Green and three of her children huddled together on the front lawn. Their faces mirrored fear and terror. Mrs. Green was hysterical.

"Theresa!" she screamed. "My Theresa is still in there!"

I've got to do something, I thought. *I've got to help.* But I stood there frozen, unable to move. Confusion and panic surrounded me, became a part of me. The whole atmosphere seemed to crackle with heat and tension. I was afraid. A great shower of fiery sparks lit the night sky as part of the house caved in, and I heard Mrs. Green scream again.

"O Lord," I prayed. "Please help me." And then I rushed to the house and pushed my way through the first available window. Once inside, I could hardly see. My heart was beating like a drum. Everything was black and smoking.

I groped my way forward until I got halfway across the room. Then abruptly, I stopped. Something—some strong and strange sensation—told me that I was in the wrong room. *This isn't right,* it seemed to say. *This isn't where you'll find her.* The feeling was so powerful that I couldn't shake it. And then, I felt on my shoulder the sure, firm grasp of a hand pulling me back toward the window.

"Get out of here!" I yelled, fearing for the other person's safety. I turned to follow, but there was no one there. There was only myself, alone and trembling.

Gasping, I headed for the window, pulled myself through, and lowered myself to the ground. I looked up to see Mrs. Green's frantic eyes desperately searching my own for encouragement. Finding none, she gestured wildly toward another window.

"There," she whispered hoarsely. "Go in there."

The window was a few feet off the ground. Someone gave me a boost, and I pushed myself inside, dropping to the floor with a thud. This room, too, was dark and smoldering. My eyes were smarting. I could barely see an arm's length ahead.

"O Lord," I prayed again, "please help me."

What happened next left me momentarily stunned. First, as if in answer to my prayer, I felt a surge of confidence that I was, indeed, in the right place, that I would find Theresa. And then, to my amazement, I felt the return of the same firm force on my shoulder that had pulled me from the other room. This time, however, it was even stronger and it seemed to push me to the floor. Though I didn't understand what was happening, I didn't fight it. Instinctively, I let it take over. Its presence was both calming and reassuring. I knew it was good.

I relaxed and let myself be pushed to the floor. I began to crawl, following the wall, arms outstretched, reaching, grabbing. I came to a bed and raised myself to search its rumpled surface. *No!* a voice seemed to warn. *Stay low!* I returned to my crawling position. I had found nothing on the bed. *Don't worry,* the voice whispered. *You're almost there. Don't worry.*

At the foot of the bed lay a great pile of charred chairs, quilts, and blankets that seemed to have been thrown to the floor by someone in a panic. Reaching deep into the tangled maze, I found what I had been looking for, an arm, a leg, it was impossible to tell—but I knew I had found Theresa. I pulled and pulled until she finally emerged, a limp little brown-haired bundle. She was badly burned.

"Theresa?" I whispered.

A shuddering gasp, barely audible, confirmed that she was alive. I threw her over my shoulder and ran for the window.

The crowd outside stared in silence as I gently laid Theresa on the ground and began to administer mouth-to-mouth resuscitation. Her small face, black with soot and burns, was expressionless. Blue lights from police cars pulsated in the darkness. As I breathed into her tiny frame, I prayed for her survival. Wailing sirens and flashing red lights announced the arrival of fire trucks. I kept on breathing and praying. I listened to the fire chief bellowing orders on his bullhorn, and then I heard the front door being kicked in. The fire, reignited by the fresh supply of oxygen, exploded with a scorching blast. Theresa's eyelids fluttered. She was breathing on her own. I held her until the ambulance arrived.

"Looks like you got her out just in time," said the medic, as he took her from my arms. "She's burned pretty bad, but she'll be all right."

I waited for the ambulance to pull away and then returned home.

Shaken by the experience, plagued by the smell of burning flesh and the echoes of terrified screams, I couldn't sleep. More than anything else, I was completely unnerved by the mysterious Presence that had led me to the little girl. I had always had faith in God and in the power of prayer, but this kind of intervention seemed uncanny, too close for comfort—at least for me. The idea was too much to comprehend, but I couldn't dismiss it. It kept me up all night.

At 7:00 A.M. I put on a jacket and shoes and returned to the scene of the fire. The house, a charred hull of blackened brick, was still smoldering. Skeletal shells of smoking furniture were strewn around the front yard. The fire inspector was there with a few policemen. He asked me what I was doing there. I told him. He said the blaze had probably been caused by a cigarette left burning on the living room sofa.

I went around to the room where I had found Theresa. Like the rest of the house, it was badly charred and blackened from smoke. The walls were blistered from the intense heat. In one corner rested the remains of a melted tennis racket.

Slowly I turned to gaze around the gutted room, when suddenly I stopped, transfixed—my eyes riveted on the wall. There, directly above the spot where I had found Theresa, was a portrait, neatly hung and, strangely, the only thing in the room undamaged by the fire. The frame, to be sure, was black with soot, but the face, the calm, steady, reassuring face, was clear and untouched.

It was a picture of Jesus.

To this day, I don't know how long I stood there, incredulously returning the portrait's gaze. But when I left, it was with new-found understanding that I whispered my thanks.

DADDY'S HAND

Macy Krupicka

When I was six years old we lived in Oklahoma City in a neighborhood where we always kept the doors locked and bolted at night. To get out the back door, Daddy had a special key that opened the dead bolt from the inside.

One night I was wakened suddenly by the sound of thunder and lightning and a torrential downpour. I rushed down the hall toward my parents' room, but was stopped by billowing smoke and flames coming from the living room. Our house had been struck by lightning.

I had to get out, but how? I couldn't reach the front door because of the flames, and the back door was locked.

On the verge of panic, I was relieved when in the darkness I felt Daddy's warm hand leading me down the hall and out the back door to our backyard. As I stood in the pouring rain, his hand let go of mine and he was gone. Frightened, I turned back to the house. There was Mom calling my name, "Macy! Macy!"

"Out here," I said. She ran out to me, and together we went around to the front, where we found Daddy with Kent, the baby, and my three-year-old sister, Amy.

"You're safe, Macy," he said, sighing with relief. Daddy told me that he had tried to get to me, but couldn't cross the flames. He had not guided me down the hall. He had not unlocked the dead bolt on the back door.

That was twelve years ago, and all these years I've never forgotten the warmth of the Hand that led me then, and leads me now, through the dark.

"*I*'VE GOT A REAL, LIVE ANGEL"

Gloria Farah

Today the river bank in La Paz, Bolivia, where our little boys, Douglas and Dennis, nearly lost their lives is covered with vines. But on that awful day in May 1965, the growth had been cut back because a new drainpipe was to be installed.

The whole family loved our jungle headquarters— loved it mostly because of the friends we'd made there. With a dozen other Wycliffe Bible Translators families, we'd started the work in this remote area. Together we'd faced crushing handicaps, struggling against indifference and hostility as we tried to translate the Bible into local tribal languages, and against mosquitoes, parasites and poisonous snakes as we tried to carve a home out of the jungle.

Because of our translation work, we were immersed day and night in the Bible. And over the months, a strange thing took place. The Bible began to *happen*. Instead of being a sacred collection of ancient stories, the Bible became an experience. We discovered that we could pray for the sick and have them get well. We experienced the fact of Christ's power over evil. And in our own family we came to know for ourselves just how real a creature a child's guardian is. Jesus tells us that a child's angel is in heaven, always looking into the face of the Father (Matthew 18:10). How important this fact became for us.

Our son Doug was seven years old, his big brother Dennis nine that spring. I remember how, on the night before the accident, my husband, David, was putting the boys to bed when Doug propped himself up on his elbow.

"Daddy, can we build a cave with our knives?"

David saw no reason to say no: How could two little boys build much of a cave with pocket knives? "Sure you can, Doug."

It wasn't, of course, until weeks later that we pieced together all that happened that next day. Doug and his older brother were playing pirates with several other mission children. They dug their cave in the cleared earth, then most of the pirates left to go swimming, leaving only Doug and Dennis and a friend named Mark at the cave entrance.

Doug saw his brother stick his head and shoulders into the shallow cave—with all their work, their tunnel went only a few feet into the dry mud bank. Doug heard Dennis' voice calling from inside the cave. "Come on in."

Doug began to crawl in. A bed of red ants had been disturbed, but the boys ignored them.

Then, with no warning, the dry mud shifted. In one instant the steep bank slid silently down on our two boys and trapped them beneath its suffocating mass.

Mark was covered too, but wiggled free and started to shout and to dig with his hands. "Dennis! Doug! Where are you?"

There was no answer, no movement. Mark began to cry for help.

Inside the cave, Doug had been slapped down on his chest. His face was smashed into the dirt, but a pocket of air helped him breathe.

"Dennis, can you hear me?"

His voice seemed to make no sound at all, but he felt a slight movement beneath him. "Dennis," Doug went on. "I can't move. I can't breathe!"

He felt another wiggle. An ant crawled onto his face, then another. The first sting came. It was on his eyelid.

"Dennis, I can't talk . . . the air's going away."

The ants were all over him now, stinging. "Dennis, I think we're maybe going to die." He began to struggle. Dirt filled his mouth.

And then Douglas stopped talking. He even stopped struggling for air. For there, next to him, was an angel. He stood bright, strong.

"Dennis!" Doug called softly, his voice relaxed. "Dennis, there's an _angel_ here. I can see him plain as anything. He's bright. He's trying to help us." Doug felt one oh-so-slight movement.

"He's not doing anything. But Dennis . . . if we die now . . . it's not so bad. . . ." Doug lost consciousness.

Up above, Mark arrived at our house screaming that Dennis and Doug had been buried. David was out in the jungle, but I ran to the cave-in. Men followed me with picks and shovels.

The slide was smooth, like a child's sand castle collapsed. The men began to probe the wet earth with sticks.

"Quick, Mark," I begged, "show the men where to dig."

Mark hurled himself down the bank. He stopped, looking around. Then, "Here!" He pointed to a spot on the earthfall. The men jumped forward. Seconds later one of the shovels touched softness. Seconds again and Doug's back and legs were free. Strong arms pulled him from the earth. Dennis' form appeared beneath him.

Neither boy was breathing. Their skin was blue. They lay on the red earth, their bodies so terribly small. Someone began to pray. Someone else ran for oxygen from the airbase.

Then Douglas moved. A moment later Dennis stirred. The oxygen arrived. We gave it to Dennis first, then to Douglas.

"Mommy!" Douglas said as soon as he opened his eyes. "Do you know what I saw? An angel."

"Shh, sweetheart. Don't try to talk yet."

By noon next day the doctor allowed the boys to get up. Another two minutes, he told us, and the lack of oxygen would have damaged the boys' brains. But because they had not spent themselves struggling, the doctor said, they had just exactly enough oxygen to come through the experience without damage. And the reason they had not struggled, all of us knew, was the angel—the angel who kept them from being afraid.

Doug lorded it over his friends all that day and for several days following. "I've got a real, live angel," Douglas said, until finally even his friend Mark had had enough.

"Oh, quit bragging, Douglas. Everybody's got a guardian angel!"

And, of course, the marvel is that Mark is right.

*I*N LOVING ARMS

Deborah C. Jacobson

The auditorium echoed with the band's rendition of "Pomp and Circumstance" as the graduating class of 1989 processed two by two into the room. My heart swelled as I recognized each one of my daughter's friends walking proudly in their royal blue caps and gowns.

And then I saw her. Tears blurred my eyes and fear threatened my composure as I watched my normally active daughter, Traci, being pushed to the front of the class in her hospital wheelchair.

My thoughts carried me back to only two days before when she was running madly through the house preparing for the long awaited overnight senior campout.

The location chosen was a remote forest campground, high in the Cascade mountains. With an elevation of approximately thirty-two hundred feet and an average late spring temperature of 30 to 40 degrees at night, even the possibility of cold rain or snow didn't dampen the spirits of the determined campers.

As she prepared to leave, I filled her with all the advice she didn't need to hear but I needed to say.

"Drive carefully. Don't put your tent too close to the campfire. Don't wander away from camp alone. And"—as I shoved an extra blanket into her arms—"have a great time, Honey."

With a smile and a roll of her eyes she kissed me good-bye, assured me she was a "big girl," and promised to be careful.

I knew Traci was a responsible teenager, but sleep wouldn't come easily to me that evening. I read for a while to try to make myself drowsy. Suddenly I felt a strong urge to pray for my daughter and her friends. Glancing at the clock on my night table, I saw it was 12:15 A.M. As I prayed, my uneasiness faded and with renewed confidence that they were in God's hands, I finally drifted off to sleep.

One hour later the phone rang. My husband answered.

"Will you accept a collect call from Pam?" the operator asked. Pam is Traci's best friend and we knew they were together.

"Hello Darwin, this is Pam," she said in a shaky voice. "Traci's okay—she hurt her leg—don't think it's broken—an accident—she's in an Aid car—meet her at Valley General hospital."

As he dressed, my husband relayed the message to me and then left for the trip to the hospital. I stayed home with our two younger children.

The silence seemed to close in around me as I watched the clock and waited for my husband to call, praying all the time and telling myself to trust in God and not to worry. There wasn't the slightest chance of sleep for me until our Traci was safely home, so I reached for my Bible, hoping to find some comfort, and randomly opened it to Jeremiah 30:17 (NAS):

"For I will restore you to health; of your wounds I will heal you says the Lord."

As I read those words, I was filled with a deep sense of calm. I knew that in that particular passage God was talking to Jeremiah about the people of Israel and Judah, but at that moment I knew God was speaking to me about my daughter and her wounds. *Why else*, I asked myself, *would He have directed me to that passage?*

What seemed like hours later, my husband's call came. Traci had no broken bones, a slight concussion, four stitches in the head and lots of cuts and bruises. He was bringing her home.

"Thank You, God." I prayed.

At about 4:00 A.M. my husband carried our bruised, but not broken, daughter into her bedroom and, together, we settled her into bed. He told me that the emergency room doctor was concerned about the immense amount of pain Traci was feeling in her left leg and had given us the phone number of an orthopedic specialist with very firm instructions to call as soon as the office opened in the morning.

Thankful that my "big girl" was safely home, I gently kissed her scraped forehead and asked, "What happened?"

"I'm not sure, Mom," she told me with a look of pain and confusion. "Ryan took his three-wheeler and was giving everyone rides up and down an old logging road. It was dark and the road was real narrow, with a steep drop off on one side, so he was driving really careful. He wasn't going fast, in fact we were going sort of slow because of the dark. As we were starting around a sharp corner something happened to the bike. Pam told me they think the front tire blew out, but all I know is that one minute I was on the back of the bike and the next minute I was flying through the air. When I fell, I hit the rocks hard and flew into the air, again. It was so dark I couldn't see anything. I couldn't stop myself, it was all rocks and air. There was nothing to stop me, Mom. I knew I was going to keep falling and falling until I hit the bottom. That's when it happened. I came down and hit the rocks again, but this time when I bounced up, someone caught me."

"Who?" I asked.

"I don't know who, Mom. I couldn't *see* anyone, but I *felt* them. I know it sounds weird, but someone caught me in the air. They caught me, Mom, and held me in their arms for a while, then they laid me down on the rocks just like they were laying me down on my bed."

As I waited for her pain medication to take effect and let her sleep, all I could think of was how grateful I was that Traci and Ryan were alive. My husband told me the cliff they plunged over was one hundred fifty feet straight down, with jagged quarry rocks lining the bank. Ryan went to the bottom with the bike, suffering only minor cuts and bruises; Traci landed just over halfway down.

It wasn't until I returned to my bed that I remembered the words of my prayer earlier that morning. At 12:15, just about the same time the accident happened, I had prayed these words, "Dear Lord, please watch over Traci and her friends. Hold her in your loving arms and keep them all safe."

"Thank You, God," I whispered once again as I closed my eyes.

The next morning, when I called the specialist, I found that the emergency room doctor had already spoken to him about Traci, and he wanted to see her as soon as we could get there. He diagnosed compartment syndrome, a rapid swelling of tissue that may cause irreversible nerve damage—the result of the severe blow to her left leg. He said he would operate on it that morning.

After coming out of the anesthesia, all Traci could think about was graduation the next evening. She was so upset that her doctor told us he would release her for two hours, and assured us that she would be all right.

The sound of applause stirred me from my musing and brought me back to the ceremony. Mothers and father, relatives and friends were cheering as their graduates were announced. As we clapped for Traci and watched her receive her diploma in her wheelchair, I realized that this was the beginning of letting go. She really was a "big girl" now, and soon she would be on her own.

With a lump in my throat I closed my eyes and silently prayed. "Thank You, God, for showing me that even when I have to let go of my children's hands I can rest in the knowledge that they will always be surrounded by Your loving arms."

AND AFTERWARDS: Traci spent eight long days in the hospital. She doesn't remember much about her graduation, being too full of painkillers, but she has the videotape her aunt took for her.

Just as I believe it was God who held my daughter on that dark mountain, I believed He continued to hold her as He directed her to three very gifted physicians.

The emergency room doctor's concerned instructions and the orthopedic surgeon's quick diagnosis kept her from having extensive nerve damage. Even the reconstructive surgeon was able to close the long incision from her knee to her ankle without any grafting because of the skilled and careful hands of the orthopedic surgeon.

Today, Traci has full use of her leg with only a small amount of numbness in one toe.

THOSE GENTLE HANDS

Joanna Rhodes-Hall

I had not thought of that young, blue-eyed nurse in years until the Sunday afternoon when my grandson, Brandon, wanted to know about his guardian angel.

The conversation started because of a gift I had given him—a picture of an angel hovering over a young boy and girl who are crossing an old, wooden bridge that looked very dangerous. I shared with him Hebrews 1:14 (TLB), "For the angels are only spirit-messengers sent out to help and care for those who are to receive salvation."

"You have an angel watching over you," I told him.

Brandon really got excited and immediately wanted to give his angel a name. As I drove him home that afternoon, he held on tightly to his "angel picture," as he calls it, and ran into the house to tell his mother that he had a guardian angel that looked after him.

Later that night I thought of *my* angel and remembered the feel of soft, gentle hands on my face—the first time almost twenty years ago. I was about to give birth to my sixth child. We had five beautiful daughters and so were praying for a son. It had been a long, hard labor for a thirty-five-year-old woman, and the time had come to be rolled into the labor room where I was carefully transferred to the delivery room bed with the funny-looking stirrups. *Why am I so apprehensive?* I remember thinking. *I've been through this five times, so it isn't like I don't know what to expect. Why is the delivery room so cold?* All the bright lights were focused down on me, but they gave off only light, no heat. The well-trained nurses and hospital personnel were scurrying about getting ready for my son's birth. But I was scared.

I closed my eyes very tightly hoping to shut out the pain and fear—and felt a cool cloth laid on my forehead and a gentle pat to the side of my head. I have never felt such gentleness in my entire life. I slowly opened my eyes and gazed into a masked face with the clearest blue eyes I have ever seen. During the delivery, she never moved from the head of my bed. When the pain became intense, her cool hands would stroke my face or head. She never spoke a word and I never saw her face without the mask.

At 1:30 P.M. on March 13, 1971, I gave birth to a nine-pound, three-ounce boy. But my joy was short-lived. As the nurse laid my son in my arms, I saw a tiny, red face that was not perfectly formed. His little nose was mashed flat and his upper lip had a large hole in it. This precious gift from God had been born with a cleft lip and palate. As tears crept out the corners of my eyes, I felt warm tears drop on my forehead and once again felt those same gentle hands on my head. But this time I sensed a slight patting motion, like a mother as she softly touches her child to comfort him as he is about to drift off to sleep.

As I was rolled out of the delivery room, I glanced back, making a quick survey of the room. I wanted to nod a thank-you to my special new friend. But I could not see her. And I never saw the nurse with the clear, blue eyes again. I asked everyone who she was, but no one could recall a nurse at the head of my bed. I even asked to see the charge nurse on duty that day in the delivery room. She said that as short-staffed as they were on that shift, it was not possible for a nurse to stand around doing nothing. She may not have been visible to anyone else, but I know that she was there with me that day. But though I have never seen her again, I have felt her presence. My son, Neal, had many operations to correct his cleft lip and palate. He had numerous ear infections, high fevers, and many sleepless nights. On the nights that I rocked and sang to him, I felt those same gentle hands on my head.

Several months ago I had some much needed surgery. Once again I had that same uneasy feeling as I was rolled quite briskly down the corridor to surgery. As the anesthesia began to take effect and I was getting very sleepy, I felt those same gentle hands on my head. I tried so hard to open my eyes, wanting to see those clear, blue eyes once more, but I was too far gone, and my eyes would not open.

In the recovery room, my first conscious thoughts were of my friend. Do you remember ever having a bad dream and being afraid to open your eyes? And then your mother takes you into her arms, rocks you, and holds you close to her. That is how I felt that day as I awoke from a drugged sleep. My friend was still there.

I am so glad I found that picture of the guardian angel watching over that little boy and girl and that I was able to give it to my oldest grandson. Because to a wide-eyed, five-year-old boy, a picture is worth a thousand words. And to me, it brings back the memory of those gentle hands.

REASSURANCE

Dear Lord:

Could You spare some Guardian Angels
    To give me peace of mind
    As my children wander from me
    And stretch the ties that bind?

    You have heavenly legions, Father.
    Could you send me just a few
    To guide my eager youngsters
    As I give them, Lord, to You?

    Oh thank You, thank You, Father,
    And, oh, my glad heart sings.
    I'm certain that just now I heard
    The swish of passing wings!

                              —Betty Banner

*I*N THE BACK OF THE TRUCK

Marion Bond West

Being a widow with teenaged boys was harder than I'd expected. My sons resented the fact that I was in charge. Sometimes I did, too.

Late one afternoon, one of my sons announced that he was going to a party he knew I'd disapprove of. I told him that he couldn't go. "I'm going anyway," Jon said defiantly. I was so tired of arguing—and then I remembered God's promise to be a husband to widows. I silently asked Him for help and thought I understood the instructions that crept into my heart. I rushed to the front porch, waved happily at my son and called out, "I'm putting some angels in the back of your truck, Jon!"

He leaned out the window. "Can you do that?" he asked with sarcasm, but I walked back to the kitchen and enjoyed the delicious flavor of *not* being in charge. God was up to something! Jon returned home shortly and stood in the kitchen watching me cook. Finally, he said, "I decided not to go to the party. What's for supper?"

I refrained from doing joyful cartwheels across the kitchen. After a pleasant supper, Jon said, half serious, half smiling, "Mother, I'm probably the only boy in Georgia with angels in the back of his truck. Would you . . . could you arrange for them to leave now?" His eye contact was good, his voice gentle.

"Certainly," I replied, smiling. I took off my apron and walked out to the porch, as though I dispatched angels on a daily routine. Jon followed. I waved toward the truck. "Thank you all very much. That's all for now. Bye."

𝒯HE FALL

Charles A. Leggett

"I felt the swish of angels' wings."

Growing up, I heard my parents recite these familiar words whenever some unexpected miracle occurred or some near tragedy was avoided. But I never really felt their true meaning until my second year of college. I attend the Virginia Military Institute, a small college nestled in the Shenandoah Valley in Virginia. During September of my third class year, the weather was still very comfortable, so one Sunday afternoon a small group of my friends and I decided to go to the nearby cliffs for some rapelling.

We arrived at the cliffs after lunch and set up our ropes. The cliffs are about one hundred twenty feet high, overlooking the Maury River. The landing area we chose was about a hundred feet below the top of the cliffs, and we rigged a safety line that led back to the top on one side. Then I decided to show off a little. Leaving the safety line, I crossed the landing area and started to climb the cliffs on my own. Like most college students my age, I hadn't given much thought to my own mortality, so I thought nothing of climbing without a safety line or even a helmet. I should have known better, because I had been rapelling and climbing several times before. But the idea of falling never entered my mind.

I started to climb the face of the cliff, moving slowly upwards, finding foot- and handholds as I climbed. I had reached within five feet of the top and was in the process of shifting my handhold, when I felt the small ledge I was standing on crumble and fall, leaving me hanging by one hand on a small outcrop of rock. Desperately I tried to find something to grab on to, but then my last handhold broke and I felt myself begin to fall. Just as I started to black out, I thought I felt a *hand* grab my arm. Then, everything went blank.

When I regained consciousness, at least five to ten minutes had passed. As I slowly became aware of my surroundings, I realized that I was sitting on a ledge with my back to the cliff, less than twenty feet above the river. My right leg was twisted painfully underneath me, and I was covered with scratches, but otherwise I was unhurt. I turned to look up the face of the cliff and found the place I had fallen from, over ninety feet above me. In my fall, my body had not only turned from facing in toward the cliff to facing outward, but I had also fallen fifteen feet diagonally across the cliff—and landed in a seated position! Dimly, I became aware of my friends calling out my name. Slowly and carefully I made my way from my ledge down to the landing area, then up the safety line to the top.

My friends were shocked when I told them what had happened. None of them could come up with a logical explanation for my safe landing. But I've never thought twice about how to explain it. You see, I was raised in a Christian home and I had always believed in the presence of guardian angels. On that Sunday afternoon, however, I met mine, and I have continuously praised God for that miracle that saved my life.

*T*HE SHINING ONES

Agnes Sanford

I am quite sure that more people see angels today than did in Abraham's day, and I could fill many chapters with stories about them.

For instance, a retired missionary in Africa, Leslie Sutton, told me this story during a conference in Lee Abbey, England. His houseboy ran to him one day in excitement saying, "The Great One is coming up the hill with all his men!" The African chieftain was not a Christian, nor was he friendly with the British in Africa. Nevertheless the little missionary (for he was indeed small compared with the great African) went forth to meet him. There he came, glorious in his robes and feathers, and with him came many men. Two of them carried a chair; they set it down and the Great One established himself therein. Then he spoke to the missionary in words somewhat like these: "Last night I saw shining ones. They came down, they went up, they came down. In my hut I have a cockatoo; they had wings like my cockatoo. One of them said to me, 'Go and see the white man on the hill, because he has the words of God.' So I am here. Speak!" The missionary spoke, and many believed him because of their chieftain who had seen in his spirit the realities of God.

This is an old story, but I will now tell you a new one, only in fact some three weeks old. A child was playing with the handle of a car door as his mother drove on a California freeway. The door flew open, and the child rolled across three lanes of traffic, all traveling at high speed. Every car stopped; no car was hurt; the child was not hurt. If you know the freeways of the Los Angeles area, you will know that this was a miracle. When the mother picked the child up, he said, "Oh, Mother, did you see them?"

"See whom?" asked the mother.

"All the angels that stopped the traffic!"

*T*HE GUARDIAN

Geneva Cobb Iijima

Whenever my husband had
to be away overnight on a
business trip, I used to be ner-
vous about staying in
the house with only our
three small children for
company.

Then came the time when
we were stationed with the
American Embassy in Japan, and
Pete was on a week-long trip. Once
again I dreaded the nights ahead until
the afternoon our six-year-old Robin
arrived home from first grade at the Navy
School nearby. In class that day she'd made a crayon
drawing of our house and she gave it to me proudly for my inspec-
tion. Yes, it had the right shape. It really did look like our house.
But what was that strange object on the top?

"It's very nice," I complimented her. "You did a good job. But
what is this?" I pointed to the odd, birdlike thing perched on the
roof.

Looking at me as if she thought me a little stupid, she casually
answered, "Why, Mama, don't you know? That's the angel taking
care of us!"

O Lord, I thought, *thank You for the faith of this little child.* Robin
knew, and I had forgotten, that He had promised to give His
angels charge over us, to keep us in all our ways (Psalm 91:11).

That evening, as I tucked the picture away with Robin's other
school mementos, my fear of the dark night was tucked away
too—buried forever.

*M*ISTY MOONLIGHT

The angels walk the floor of heaven tonight,
Their garments trailing splendor as they pass;
A rapture tips the thin green leaves with light,
And showers quivering gold upon the grass;
The slender poplars shake their silver lace
Against the trembling glory of the stars;
The old earth is a feathered thing of grace,
Unmindful of a million ancient scars.

The look of heaven is on the land and sea,
And something in this pale celestial light
Has loosed my yoke of weariness from me,
And set my spirit winging, free and white,
The old, old hurt my heart has borne so long
Grows faint and dim as some forgotten song.

—Grace Noll Crowell

III

ANGELS EVERLASTING

Friends Angelical

Far beyond the shifting screen
Made of things that can be seen,
Are our friends angelical
Of the Land Celestial.

Thence they come to tend the flowers
That we thought were only ours.
What their toils we may not know,
As they come and as they go.

Only this we know: they see
As we cannot, what shall be,
Watch the hidden buds unfold,
Dream of colour, heart of gold.

Therefore look behind the screen,
Trust the powers of the Unseen.
Neither vague nor mystical
Are our friends angelical.

—Amy Carmichael

III

*A*NGELS EVERLASTING

Here is a gathering of heavenly beings you already know from
your Bible-reading. These are some of the many angels who appear
throughout the Old and New Testaments and provide us with the
insight so vital to understanding the nature and function of the
angels who are with us today. Some of them, like Gabriel and
Michael, have names; most do not, but all of them have their
appointed tasks. They are the ministering spirits who can assume
many forms. Their home is in heaven, yet their ministry is on
earth. Indeed, they exist for us.

   As you read about them now, remember that these are but a few
of the angels mentioned in the Bible. A good starting point for a
deeper study would be a reading of Ezekiel 1 and 10 and
Revelation 4. For the present, however, as you look at the various
roles and missions of biblical angels, let your mind reach out to the
angels whose stories have been collected in this book. Think about
the parallels between the two, ancient and modern. Then let yourself take a flight of fancy with the tantalizing idea that the vast
array of heavenly hosts, all of whom reside in eternity, are all the
same angels of the Lord who are among us today.

$\mathscr{A}$NGELS AT THE BEGINNING . . .

*Angels first appear in the Biblical record as guardians of the Garden of
Eden—to keep the first man and woman out, and away from the Tree of Life.*

To Adam (God) said, "Because you listened to your wife and ate from
the tree about which I commanded you, 'You must not eat of it,'
   "Cursed is the ground because of you;
   through painful toil you will eat of it
   all the days of your life. . . ."

. . . And the Lord God said, "The man has now become like one of us, knowing good and evil. He must not be allowed to reach out his hand and take also from the tree of life and eat, and live forever." So the Lord God banished him from the Garden of Eden to work the ground from which he had been taken. After he drove the man out, he placed on the east side of the Garden of Eden cherubim, and a flaming sword flashing back and forth to guard the way to the tree of life.

—Genesis 3:17, 22–24, NIV

. . . AND THE 𝒞ND

The last mention of angels in the Bible comes in connection with the revelation to John of the eternal City of God, our future home, and the Tree of Life now available to heal humans from their sin, evil and sickness.

Then I saw a new heaven and a new earth, for the first heaven and the first earth had passed away. . . . And I saw the Holy City, the new Jerusalem, coming down out of heaven from God, prepared as a bride beautifully dressed for her husband. And I heard a loud voice from the throne saying, "Now the dwelling of God is with men, and he will live with them." . . .

One of the seven angels who had the seven bowls full of the seven last plagues came and said to me, "Come, I will show you the bride, the wife of the Lamb." And he carried me away in the Spirit to a mountain great and high, and showed me the Holy City, Jerusalem, coming down out of the heaven from God. . . . I did not see a temple in the city, because the Lord God Almighty and the Lamb are its temple. The city does not need the sun or the moon to shine on it, for the glory of God gives it light, and the Lamb is its lamp. . . . Nothing impure will ever enter it, nor will anyone who does what is shameful or deceitful, but only those whose names are written in the Lamb's book of life.

Then the angel showed me the river of the water of life, as clear as crystal, flowing from the throne of God and of the Lamb down the middle of the great street of the city. On each side of the river stood the tree of life, bearing twelve crops of fruit, yielding its fruit every month. And the leaves of the tree are for the healing of the nations. No longer will there be any curse. . . .

The angel said to me. "These words are trustworthy and true. The Lord, the God of the spirits of the prophets, sent his angel to show his servants the things that must soon take place."

—Revelation 21:1–3, 9–10, 22–23, 27; 22:1–3, 6, NIV

*T*HE NATURE OF ANGELS

Angels are spiritual beings, without earthly, material bodies, which is why they appear to human beings in many different forms. Often they are surrounded by brilliant light, and their appearance inspires great fear and awe. They have tremendous powers, but they are created beings, and therefore humans are not to worship them, since we, too, are God's creation, and only "a little lower than the angels."

Bless the Lord, O my soul. . . . Who maketh his angels spirits; his ministers a flaming fire.

—Psalm 104:1,4

When [God] . . . brings the firstborn into the world, He says:

"Let all the angels of God worship Him."

And of the angels He says:

"Who makes His angels spirits
And His ministers a flame of fire."

But to the Son He says:

"Your throne, O God, is forever and ever;
A scepter of righteousness is the scepter of Your Kingdom. . . ."

And:

"You, Lord, in the beginning laid the foundation of the earth,
And the heavens are the work of Your hands;
They will perish, but You remain;
And they will all grow old like a garment;
Like a cloak You will fold them up,
And they will be changed.
But You are the same,
And Your years will not fail."

But to which of the angels has He ever said:

"Sit at My right hand,
Till I make Your enemies Your footstool"?

Are they not all ministering spirits sent forth to minister for those who will inherit salvation?

—Hebrews 1:1–14, NKJV
(see also Hebrews 2:5–9)

Don't let anyone declare you lost when you refuse to worship angels, as they say you must. . . . These proud men . . . are not connected to Christ.

—Colossians 2:18–19, 6, TLB

Jesus replied [to a trick question put to him by the Sadducees], "The people of this age marry and are given in marriage. But those who are considered worthy of taking part in that age and in the resurrection from the dead will neither marry nor be given in marriage, and they can no longer die; for they are like the angels. They are God's children, since they are children of the resurrection."

—Luke 20:34–36, NIV

[The angel who rolled away the great stone from the doorway of the tomb where Jesus was buried had an] appearance . . like lightning, and his clothes were white as snow. The guards were so afraid of him that they shook and became like dead men.

—Matthew 28:3–4, NIV

✐NGELS AT THE DOOR

Do not neglect to show hospitality to strangers, for thereby some have entertained angels unawares.

—Hebrews 13:2, RSV

Throughout the Old Testament particularly, God and His angels appear to people looking sometimes like ordinary human beings, but sometimes with enough of a difference that the people suspect God's presence. Perhaps the most famous example of entertaining angels unawares is the time Abraham invited three strangers to stop in their journey and share a meal with him.

The Lord appeared again to Abraham while he was living in the oak grove at Mamre. This is the way it happened: One hot summer afternoon as he was sitting in the opening of his tent, he suddenly noticed three men coming toward him. He sprang up and ran to meet them and welcomed them.

"Sirs," he said, "please don't go any further. Stop awhile and rest here in the shade of this tree while I get water to refresh your feet, and a bite to eat to strengthen you. Do stay awhile before continuing your journey."

"All right," they said, "do as you have said."

Then Abraham ran back to the tent and said to Sarah, "Quick! Mix up some pancakes! Use your best flour, and make enough for the three of them!" Then he ran out to the herd and selected a fat calf and told a servant to hurry and butcher it. Soon, taking them cheese and milk and the roast veal, he set it before the men and stood beneath the trees beside them as they ate.

"Where is Sarah, your wife?" they asked him.

"In the tent," Abraham replied.

Then the Lord said, "Next year I will give you and Sarah a son!" (Sarah was listening from the tent door behind him.) Now Abraham and Sarah were both very old,* and Sarah was long since past the time when she could have a baby.

*Abraham was ninety-nine and Sarah eighty-nine (see Genesis 23:1, 17:17).

So Sarah laughed silently. "A woman my age have a baby?" she scoffed to herself. "And with a husband as old as mine?"

Then God said to Abraham, "Why did Sarah laugh? Why did she say 'Can an old woman like me have a baby?' Is anything too hard for God? Next year, just as I told you, I will certainly see to it that Sarah has a son."

—Genesis 18:1–14, TLB

Judge 13 tells the story of the angel who predicted Samson's birth to his mother and his father, but only after they offered him a meal, and he told them instead to burn it as a sacrifice, did they recognize him as an angel, because he ascended heavenward in the flames.

*Æ*NGELS AT BIRTH

When a special child is to be born, a child important to the fate of God's people, God sends an angel to announce the child's coming. In the New Testament we are told the name of this angel: Gabriel.

In the time of Herod king of Judea there was a priest named Zechariah, who belonged to the priestly division of Abijah; his wife Elizabeth was also a descendant of Aaron. Both of them were upright in the sight of God, observing all the Lord's commandments. . . . But they had no children, because Elizabeth was barren; and they were both well along in years.

Once when Zechariah's division was on duty and he was serving as a priest before God, he was chosen by lot, according to the custom of the priesthood, to go into the temple of the Lord and burn incense. And when the time for the burning of incense came, all the assembled worshipers were praying outside.

Then an angel of the Lord appeared to him, standing at the right side of the altar of incense. When Zechariah saw him, he was startled and was gripped with fear. But the angel said to him: "Do not be afraid, Zechariah: your prayer has been heard. Your wife Elizabeth will bear you a son, and you are to give him the name John. . . ."

Zechariah asked the angel, "How can I be sure of this? I am an old man and my wife is well along in years."

The angel answered, "I am Gabriel. I stand in the presence of God, and I have been sent to speak to you and to tell you this good news. And now you will be silent and not be able to speak until the day this happens, because you did not believe my words, which will come true at their proper time."

. . . When his time of service was completed, he returned home. After this his wife Elizabeth became pregnant and for five months remained in seclusion. "The Lord has done this for me," she said. "In these days he has shown his favor and taken away my disgrace among the people."

In the sixth month [of Elizabeth's pregnancy], God sent the angel Gabriel to Nazareth, a town in Galilee, to a virgin pledged to be married to a man named Joseph, a descendant of David. The virgin's name was Mary. The angel went to her and said, "Greetings, you who are highly favored! The Lord is with you."

Mary was greatly troubled at his words and wondered what kind of greeting this might be. But the angel said to her, "Do not be afraid, Mary, you have found favor with God. You will be with child and give birth to a son, and you are to give him the name Jesus. He will be great and will be called the Son of the Most High. The Lord God will give him the throne of his father David, and he will reign over the house of Jacob forever; his kingdom will never end."

"How will this be," Mary asked the angel, "since I am a virgin?"

The angel answered, "The Holy Spirit will come upon you, and the power of the Most High will overshadow you. So the holy one to be born will be called the Son of God. Even Elizabeth your relative is going to have a child in her old age, and she who was said to be barren is in her sixth month. For nothing is impossible with God."

"I am the Lord's servant," Mary answered. "May it be to me as you have said." Then the angel left her.

—Luke 1:5–38, NIV

ÆNGELS AT DEATH

The image of angels coming to escort a dying saint into the presence of God is based on a story Jesus told, the story of the rich man (also known as Dives, from the Latin word for "rich") and Lazarus. Lazarus, a beggar covered with sores, spent his days at the gate of the rich man. "Abraham's side" or "bosom" (KJV) to which Jesus refers in His story, was the name given to Paradise in Jesus' day. You can read the whole story in Luke 16:19–31.

"The time came when the beggar died and the angels carried him to Abraham's side."

—Luke 16:22, NIV

*C*ARRIED BY ANGELS

"Carried by angels"—it is all we know
Of how they go;
We heard it long ago.
It is enough; they are not lonely there,
Lost nestlings blown about in fields of air.
The angels carry them; the way, they know.
Our kind Lord told us so.

—Amy Carmichael

*A*NGELS AT REBIRTH AND RESURRECTION

Since all angels are "ministering spirits sent to serve those who will inherit salvation" (Hebrews 1:14, NIV), they are concerned over what happens to human beings, how we respond to God's offer of love and salvation.

Then Jesus told them this parable: "Suppose one of you has a hundred sheep and loses one of them. Does he not leave the ninety-nine in the open country and go after the lost sheep until he finds it? And when he finds it, he joyfully puts it on his shoulders and goes home. Then he calls his friends and neighbors together and says, 'Rejoice with me: I have found my lost sheep.' I tell you that in the same way there will be more rejoicing in heaven over one sinner who repents than over ninety-nine righteous persons who do not need to repent.

"Or suppose a woman has ten silver coins and loses one. Does she not light a lamp, sweep the house and search carefully until she finds it? And when she finds it, she calls her friends and neighbors together and says, 'Rejoice with me; I have found my lost coin.' In the same way, I tell you, there is rejoicing in the presence of the angels of God over one sinner who repents."

—Luke 15:3–10, NIV

For the Lord himself will come down from heaven, with a loud command, with the voice of the archangel and with the trumpet call of God, and the dead in Christ will rise first. After that, we who are still alive and are left will be caught up with them in the clouds to meet the Lord in the air. And so we will be with the Lord forever.

—1 Thessalonians 4:16–17, NIV

ANGELS AND THE LIFE OF JESUS

Angels are uniquely associated with the whole life and ministry of Jesus— and His death and resurrection. We have already read of Gabriel's announcement to Mary of His birth.

This is how the birth of Jesus Christ came about. His mother Mary was pledged to be married to Joseph, but before they came together, she was found to be with child through the Holy Spirit. Because Joseph her husband was a righteous man and did not want to expose her to public disgrace, he had in mind to divorce her quietly.

But after he had considered this, an angel of the Lord appeared to him in a dream and said, "Joseph son of David, do not be afraid to take Mary home as your wife, because what is conceived in her is from the Holy Spirit. She will give birth to a son, and you are to give him the name Jesus, because he will save his people from their sins." . . .

When Joseph woke up, he did what the angel of the Lord had commanded him. . . .

—Matthew 1:18–21, 24, NIV

And there were shepherds living out in the fields nearby [Bethlehem], keeping watch over their flocks at night. An angel of the Lord appeared to them, and the glory of the Lord shone around them, and they were terrified. But the angel said to them, "Do not be afraid. I bring you good news of great joy that will be for all the people. Today in the town of David a Savior has been born to you; he is Christ the Lord. This will be a sign to you: You will find a baby wrapped in clothes and lying in a manger."

[And for the angelic choir, see the section "The Heavenly Hosts" later in this chapter.]

—Luke 2:8–12 NIV

When [the Magi] had gone, an angel of the Lord appeared to
Joseph in a dream. "Get up," he said, "take the child and his mother
and escape to Egypt. Stay there until I tell you, for Herod is going
to search for the child to kill him."

So he got up, took the child and his mother during the night
and left for Egypt. . . .

After Herod died, an angel of the Lord appeared in a dream to
Joseph in Egypt and said, "Get up, take the child and his mother
and go to the land of Israel, for those who were trying to take the
child's life are dead."

So he got up, took the child and his mother and went to the
land of Israel.

—Matthew 2:13–14,19–21 NIV

[After his baptism] Jesus was led by the Spirit into the desert to
be tempted by the devil. After fasting forty days and forty nights,
he was hungry. The tempter came to him and said, "If you are the
Son of God, tell these stones to become bread."

Jesus answered, "It is written: 'Man does not live on bread alone,
but on every word that comes from the mouth of God.'"

[After two more major temptations] Jesus said to him, "Away
from me, Satan! For it is written: 'Worship the Lord your God, and
serve him only,'"

Then the devil left him, and angels came and attended him.

—Matthew 4:1–4, 10–11, NIV

[From the Upper Room, after the Last Supper with the disciples]
Jesus went out as usual to the Mount of Olives, and his disciples
followed him. On reaching the place, he said to them, "Pray that
you will not fall into temptation." He withdrew about a stone's
throw beyond them, knelt down and prayed, "Father, if you are
willing, take this cup from me; yet not my will, but yours be done."
An angel from heaven appeared to him and strengthened him. And
being in anguish, he prayed more earnestly, and his sweat was like
drops of blood falling to the ground.

—Luke 22:39–44, NIV

[After Jesus had been crucified and put in Joseph of Arimathea's tomb on Friday, and] after the Sabbath, at dawn on the first day of the week, Mary Magdalene and the other Mary went to look at the tomb.

There was a violent earthquake, for an angel of the Lord came down from heaven and, going to the tomb, rolled back the stone and sat on it.

—Matthew 28:1–2, NIV

On the first day of the week, very early in the morning, the women took the spices they had prepared and went to the tomb. They found the stone rolled away from the tomb, but when they entered, they did not find the body of the Lord Jesus. While they were wondering about this, suddenly two men in clothes that gleamed like lightning stood beside them. In their fright the women bowed down with their faces to the ground, but the men said to them, "Why do you look for the living among the dead? He is not here; he has risen!"

—Luke 24:1–6, NIV

[Jesus] appeared to them over a period of forty days and spoke about the kingdom of God. . . . "You will receive power when the Holy Spirit comes on you; and you will be my witnesses. . . ."

After he said this, he was taken up before their very eyes, and a cloud hid him from their sight.

They were looking intently up in the sky as he was going, when suddenly two men dressed in white stood beside them. "Men of Galilee," they said, "why do you stand here looking into the sky? This same Jesus, who has been taken from you into heaven, will come back in the same way you have seen him go into heaven."

—Acts 1:3, 8–11, NIV

🅐 SHINING HOPE

God grant that all who watch today
　Beside their sepulchers of loss,
May find the great stone rolled away,—
　May see at last, with vision clear,
　The shining angel standing near,
And through the dimly lighted soul
Again may joy's evangel roll
　The glory of the Cross.

—Julia H. Thayer

*C*OMMISSIONING ANGELS

The angel of the Lord came and sat down under the oak in Ophrah that belonged to Joash the Abiezrite, where his son Gideon was threshing wheat in a wine-press to keep it from the Midianites. When the angel of the Lord appeared to Gideon, he said, "The Lord is with you, mighty warrior."

—Judges 6:11–12, NIV

The Bible records that when God had a special work for a person to do, He often sent an angel, sometimes in a vision, sometimes in waking hours, to call that person to the task. From a human point of view, the choice might have seemed an unlikely one, but God's call and commissioning produced the person He could use. Gideon was a farmer, afraid of the marauding Midianites, not a fearless warrior. But through God's call, he became a mighty warrior, who defeated the Midianites. (See Judges 6 & 7.) Here are some other examples of the commissioning of angels.

Now when Joshua was near Jericho, he looked up and saw a man standing in front of him with a drawn sword in his hand. Joshua went up to him and asked, "Are you for us or for our enemies?"

"Neither," he replied, "but as commander of the army of the Lord I have now come." Then Joshua fell facedown to the ground in reverence, and asked him, "What message does my Lord have for his servant?"

The commander of the Lord's army replied, "Take off your sandals, for the place where you are standing is holy." . . .

Then the Lord said to Joshua, "See, I have delivered Jericho into your hands. . . ."

—Joshua 5:13–15, 6:2, NIV

In the year that King Uzziah died, I saw the Lord seated on a throne, high and exalted, and the train of his robe filled the temple. Above him were seraphs, each with six wings: With two wings they covered their faces, with two they covered their feet, and with two they were flying. And they were calling to one another:
"Holy, holy, holy is the Lord Almighty;
the whole earth is full of his glory."
. . . "Woe to me!" I cried. "I am ruined! For I am a man of unclean lips, and I live among a people of unclean lips, and my eyes have seen the King, the Lord Almighty."

Then one of the seraphs flew to me with a live coal in his hand, which he had taken with tongs from the altar. With it he touched my mouth and said, "See, this has touched your lips; your guilt is taken away and your sin atoned for."

Then I heard the voice of the Lord saying, "Whom shall I send? And who will go for us?"

And I said, "Here am I. Send me!"

—Isaiah 6:1–8, NIV

*A*NGELS AT THE JUDGMENT

As God's servants, angels both announce judgment on evil and also execute it. We first meet angels in judgment in connection with the city of Sodom, when they announced to Abraham the fate of Sodom and then appeared to Lot, Abraham's nephew, in the city and led him and his family to safety (Genesis 18 & 19). Angels will also have a part in the final judgment of human beings. Jesus told several parables relating to this judgment which will come at the end of the age. One of them, the parable of the tares or weeds, told about a man who found that someone had sown bad seed in his field of wheat. Tare, or darnel plants, look exactly like wheat until the heads have ripened, so when the man's servants wanted to pull up the weeds, the owner said, no, wait until the harvest (Matthew 13:24–30).

[Jesus'] disciples came to him and said, "Explain to us the parable of the weeds in the field."

He answered, "The one who sowed the good seed is the Son of Man. The field is the world, and the good seed stands for the sons of the kingdom. The weeds are the sons of the evil one, and the enemy who sows them is the devil. The harvest is the end of the age, and the harvesters are angels.

"As the weeds are pulled up and burned in the fire, so it will be at the end of the age. The Son of Man will send out his angels, and they will weed out of his kingdom everything that causes sin and all who do evil. . . . "

—Matthew 13:36–41, 47–50, NIV

The Book of Revelation is full of John's vision of angels pouring out on the earth God's final judgment on evil and wickedness. Here are a few examples.

And I saw the seven angels who stand before God, and to them were given seven trumpets. . . . Then the seven angels who had the seven trumpets prepared to sound them.

The first angel sounded his trumpet, and there came hail and fire mixed with blood, and it was hurled down upon the earth. A third of the earth was burned up, a third of the trees were burned up, and all the green grass was burned up.

The second angel sounded his trumpet, and something like a huge mountain, all ablaze, was thrown into the sea. A third of the sea turned into blood, a third of the living creatures in the sea died, and a third of the ships were destroyed.

The third angel sounded his trumpet, and a great star, blazing like a torch, fell from the sky on a third of the rivers and on the springs of water—the name of the star is Wormwood. A third of the waters turned bitter, and many people died. . . .

The fourth angel sounded his trumpet, and a third of the sun was struck, a third of the moon, and a third of the stars, so that a third of them turned dark. A third of the day was without light, and also a third of the night.

—Revelation 8:2–12, NIV

I saw in heaven another great and marvelous sign: seven angels with the seven last plagues—last, because with them God's wrath is completed.

—Revelation 15:1, NIV

There will come a time, however, when human beings will have a part in judging angels. The Apostle Paul is the one who tells us this, in a letter to the Corinthian Christians. He is chiding the Christians for taking the lawsuits to the pagan courts, rather than judging the cases themselves.

If any of you has a dispute with another, dare he take it before the ungodly for judgment instead of before the saints [Christians]? Do you not know that the saints will judge the world? And if you are to judge the world, are you not competent to judge trivial cases? Do you not know that we will judge angels? How much more the things of this life!

—1 Corinthians 6:1–3, niv

_T_HE HEAVENLY HOSTS

ANGELS OF WAR

The chariots of God are twenty thousand,
even thousands of angels:
the Lord is among them, as in Sinai,
in the holy place.

      —Psalm 68:17

One of the names of God in the Old Testament
is Lord of Hosts, that is, the commander of the
armies of heaven. The first mention of these
hosts of angels comes in connection with Jacob,
Abraham's grandson. Jacob first met them in a
dream, while he was running from his angry
twin Esau. Many years, two wives, at least
eleven children, and many herds of cattle and
sheep later, he met the hosts again, just before he
was reunited with Esau. The Lord's hosts are poised to war against the
powers of evil—Satan and his fallen angels. The angelic commander of the
hosts of heaven is Michael, called the archangel in Jude 9.

So Jacob left Beer-sheba and journeyed toward Haran. That night,
when he stopped to camp at sundown, he found a rock for a headrest and lay down to sleep, and dreamed that a staircase reached
from earth to heaven, and he saw the angels of God going up and
down upon it.

At the top of the stairs stood the Lord. . . .

Then Jacob woke up. "God lives here!" he exclaimed in terror.
"I've stumbled into his home! This is the awesome entrance to
heaven!" The next morning he got up very early and set his stone
headrest upright as a memorial pillar, and poured olive oil over it.
He named the place Bethel ("House of God").

      —Genesis 28:10–13, 16–19, TLB

Jacob went on his way [after parting amicably with his frustrated father-in-law Laban] and the angels of God met him; and when Jacob saw them he said, "This is God's army!" So he called the name of that place Mahanaim [meaning "Two Armies"].

—Genesis 32:1–2, RSV

[When Jesus was arrested, one of the disciples] reached for his sword, drew it out and struck the servant of the high priest, cutting off his ear.

"Put your sword back in its place," Jesus said to him, "for all who draw the sword will die by the sword. Do you think I cannot call on my Father, and he will at once put at my disposal more than twelve legions of angels? But how then would the Scriptures be fulfilled that say it must happen in this way?"

—Matthew 26:51–54, NIV

Now war rose in heaven, Michael and his angels fighting against the dragon; and the dragon and his angels fought, but they were defeated and there was no longer any place for them in heaven.

—Revelation 12:7–8, RSV

Then I saw heaven opened, and behold, a white horse! He who sat upon it is called Faithful and True, and in righteousness he judges and makes war. . . . And the armies of heaven, arrayed in fine linen, white and pure, followed him on white horses.

—Revelation 19:11–14, RSV

ANGELS OF PRAISE

The hosts of heaven aren't always involved with war. One of their many tasks is that of praise. The biblical writers show angels as well as humans praising God, and call on them and us to persist in that activity. Perhaps the most well-known occasion for angels' praise is at the birth of Jesus, God's Son. And we will join them for all eternity, praising God in heaven for his marvelous works and for our salvation.

The Lord has established his throne in the heavens,
    and his kingdom rules over all.
Bless the Lord, O you his angels,
    you mighty ones who do his word,
    hearkening to the voice of his word!
Bless the Lord, all his hosts,
    his ministers that do his will!
Bless the Lord, all his works,
    in all places of his dominion.
Bless the Lord, O my soul!

—Psalm 103:19–22, RSV

Praise the Lord!
Praise the Lord from the heavens,
    praise him in the heights!
Praise him, all his angels,
    praise him, all his host!

—Psalm 148:1–2, RSV

Suddenly, the angel [announcing the birth of Jesus] was joined by a vast host of others—the armies of heaven—praising God:

"Glory to God in the highest heaven," they sang, "and peace on earth for all those pleasing him."

When this great army of angels had returned again to heaven, the shepherds said to each other, "Come on! Let's go to Bethlehem! Let's see this wonderful thing that has happened, which the Lord has told us about."

—Luke 2:13–15, TLB

You have come right up into Mount Zion, to the city of the living God, the heavenly Jerusalem, and to the gathering of countless
happy angels; and to the church, composed of all those registered
in heaven; and to God who is Judge of all; and to the spirits of the
redeemed in heaven, already made perfect; and to Jesus himself,
who has brought us his wonderful new agreement. . . .

—Hebrews 12:22–24, TLB

After this I looked, and lo, in heaven an open door! . . . And lo, a
throne stood in heaven, with one seated on the throne! . . . Then I
looked, and I heard around the throne . . . the voice of many
angels, numbering myriads of myriads and thousands of thousands,
saying with a loud voice, "Worthy is the Lamb who was slain, to
receive power and wealth and wisdom and might and honor and
glory and blessing!" . . .

After this I looked, and behold, a great multitude . . . from every
nation, from all tribes and peoples and tongues, standing before the
throne and before the Lamb, clothed in white robes, with palm
branches in their hands, and crying out with a loud voice,
"Salvation belongs to our God who sits upon the throne, and to the
Lamb!" And all the angels stood round the throne and round the
elders and the four living creatures, and they fell on their faces
before the throne and worshiped God, saying, "Amen! Blessing and
glory and wisdom and thanksgiving and honor and power and
might be to our God for ever and ever! Amen."

—Revelation 4:1–2; 5:11–12; 7:9–12, RSV

IV

ANGELS AT LARGE

Nameless Saints

The healing of the world
Is in its nameless saints. Each separate star
Means nothing, but a myriad scattered stars
Break up the night and make it beautiful.

—Bayard Taylor

IV

ANGELS AT LARGE

So far in this book you have met those angels who guard us from danger or who drift in and out of our lives to help at fortuitous moments. All of those stories have dealt with dramatic, often desperate situations. Now, keeping in mind that God has seen to it that His charges come to us in a variety of forms and guises, it is time to meet another kind of angel—and there are legions of them everywhere.

You'll find little that is spectacular about these angels. Their wings are not apparent. They shine with an inner, not outer, glow. They are as easy to be with as an old-shoe friend, so human that it would never enter your mind that they are in fact messengers from heaven. Angelic they may be, but angels, no.

Are you certain?

Pause a moment and reflect. Think back over the people you have known who have changed your life for the better. Think of the child, the friend, the teacher who by their presence created an atmosphere of love. Is it so difficult to believe that an almighty God sent them on a mission—to you?

In the one rugged adventure story in this chapter, "Angels over the Atlantic," an Air Force Major named James Sills begins to ponder the danger he has just lived through. "Maybe when we face the impossible," he says to himself, "He gives us angels too, real ones."

Major Sills is just beginning to consider the possibility that real people can be real angels.

Once you have closed this book and have sat back to muse about what you have read, you and Major Sills will have something in common.

$\mathscr{T}$HREE TIMES AN ANGEL

Oscar Greene

Recently I read a story about a man who believed that a ministering angel appeared to him at significant moments in his life. I have the same belief about certain people—especially the stranger who appeared at my father's funeral.

Father died in 1942, during the war, and I traveled the nine hundred miles by train from Rock Island Arsenal to my boyhood home of Williamstown, Massachusetts. At the chapel there was a young man standing in the back. Later I discovered he was from the fraternity where my father had worked.

In 1971 my wife and I drove six hundred miles from our home in Massachusetts to Canton, Ohio, for our son's wedding. After the ceremony I chatted with the minister, who warmly recalled his college days in my home state. Only later did my son learn that this man was the stranger who had attended my father's funeral.

Then in 1977 I made another journey when my mother died. The funeral services were held on Staten Island in New York, where Mother had lived for many years. Afterward my wife and I accompanied Mother's body back to Williamstown, where she would be buried next to my father.

The words the minister spoke at mother's graveside were some of the most comforting I had ever heard. And who was that minister? He was the stranger at my father's funeral, the pastor who had married my son and his wife. And now he was the new pastor of my boyhood church.

*O*RACLE IN AN APRON

Helen Margaret Younger

I've never been sure why age sixteen is called "sweet." It's an age when many youngsters hide uncertainty about handling grown-up life by adopting a cocky, cynical attitude and by putting down most of the conventions as square. That's the way I was, at any rate. When I was sixteen, World War II had just ended and kids had that "live fast, tomorrow may not come" attitude. And I had definitely decided to leave our "hick town" in New England and give swift living a try as soon as I graduated from high school.

Meanwhile, I was old enough to look for a summer job. Two friends had worked in a local hotel the previous summer and they were going back, so I applied, too. One opening was left, as a waitress in the coffee shop. I was told to report there and ask for Heggy, the veteran waitress and woman in charge.

Heggy? The funny sort of name turned out to fit its owner. A small, wrinkled, homely woman with a nest of rust-gray hair and round, owlish, horn-rimmed glasses, Heggy could have been the wife of an elderly elf.

"I was told to report to you?" I said, my voice heavy with question marks.

She looked at me and smiled. "Wonderful," she said cheerfully. And with that, though I didn't know it, my real growing up began.

The hotel was busy, and for some of the girls under Heggy this was a first job. We forgot orders and bumped into each other, making more work than we got done. Heggy never lost her temper. She helped mop up spilled coffee or pick up the pieces of a broken dish. "No sense getting angry unless it changes things," she'd say. "I know you'll be more careful next time." She was quick to lend a hand when we were rushed, but never pushed us to hurry. Day after day she spoke cheerful, encouraging words. She kidded with the busboys and dishwashers and told them how handsome they were. When the girls complained about our "dreary" black-and-white uniforms, Heggy bought bright red aprons for us. "Pretty young girls need color," she said.

In the coffee shop kitchen I noticed a glass jar filled with money on top of the dishwasher. I asked a second-year girl about it. "Oh, that's Heggy's tip jar," she said. "She leaves it there for us. You take what you need and put back what you can."

"You're kidding," I said. "How does she know what goes back?"

"She doesn't. She trusts us."

Slowly, without realizing it, we began to shape up into a pretty efficient staff. Heggy's trust in us was so complete that she encouraged our confidence in one another—and ourselves. But her good will wasn't reserved for the coffee shop employees.

Heggy knew every one of the townspeople who came in. "How's your leg healing?" she'd ask, or, "Did you get the job?" She had been widowed at a young age and these people were her family. One was a local boy, recently back from the Army and newly married. John was starting a career as a salesman and not doing well. Heggy knew that he and his bride were struggling to make ends meet, and she saw that his confidence in himself was sagging. One morning as he sat forlornly over coffee, she said, "John, I'll make a deal with you. Any day this month that you get three orders before noon, we'll celebrate with lunch on the house." By the end of the month he was eating free every day, and his sales career was on its way.

One day I asked Heggy how she got her name. She laughed. "It's a strange one, isn't it? I did it to myself. My name is Helga, but when I was little I couldn't pronounce the letter l, so I called myself Hegga. My family slurred it to Heggy and that's all I was ever called at home." She grinned at me, "Kinda fits an old character like me, don't you think?" My cheeks burned as I remembered my first impression of her. *How easy it is to misjudge.*

Heggy had no children, but considered most of the kids in town part hers. Often they brought their troubles to her to "rehearse" before talking them out at home. She never pried into anyone's affairs, yet she smoothed the paths between parents and offspring and husbands and wives. Strangers benefited, too, Travel-weary children glowed when Heggy handed out materials from her own supply of coloring books and crayons and asked for a special picture to hang on the wall. Families often stopped back on their return trip just to see her. She had a favorite saying: "There are plenty of thorns in life. You have to remember to look for the roses."

I'm not sure when it was that I found myself offering to help Heggy every chance I got, but by the end of the summer I know that I was a less thorny person—ready to look for roses myself. I had drifted along during my first two years of high school and I decided I'd really study and do better. I did—and I also found I was enjoying my family more, along with my town and its people.

Heggy moved to Florida to live with her sister the next spring, and we wrote to each other until she died several years later.

Nearly four decades have passed since my sixteenth summer—years when I married and raised three children—yet the memory of Heggy is as fresh as the roses she loved to remind me of. And no wonder. The woman with the funny name was a waitress who "served" in the spirit of Jesus Christ, a teacher who showed me how to make life sweet at any age.

NOT PART OF THE JOB

Elisa Vazquez

Brrriiinng. Brriinng. I looked with annoyance at the telephone ringing on my desk. It was 7:20 A.M., more than an hour before the start of the business day and I was the only soul in the airline's office.

Brriinng. Later I would think of that sound as the starting bell for the most significant journey of my twenty-five years; a journey in miles and an inward journey. But at that moment I ignored it and soon the noisy signal cut off.

I enjoyed getting to work early. It gave me a quiet time to sip hot chocolate and relax before starting another day as a supervisor of passenger services. I felt I needed a peaceful start—my job often called for soothing those customers known in the trade as "irates." Now, as I settled back to read my newspaper, the phone jangled again. Once more I let it go unanswered.

Five minutes passed. My hot chocolate had reached the perfect drinking temperature. I was lifting my cup when my phone began ringing a third time. For some reason I decided to count the rings: 21, 22, 23 . . . 34. The persistence of the caller got the best of me and I picked up the receiver. "Good morning. Miss Vazquez speaking," I said, thinking it was not a good morning at all.

"Miss Vazquez, I've been trying to reach you." The voice was male, with the timbre of stress in it.

"The office opens at eight-thirty," I began, but the caller interrupted.

"I'm sorry to call so early, but I have a problem and I was told to talk to you. My name is Ashly.*"

Annoyed that he had completely ignored what I had said about office hours, I took a swallow of my hot chocolate, now cold, and made a face. "I'll help if I can, Mr. Ashly."

*The name has been changed.

"I have a young grandson in Los Angeles who needs to fly to New York by himself."

"That's no problem," I answered quickly. "I'll give you our reservations number. Just call and arrange to prepay your grandson's ticket in New York for his flight from—"

Again the man interrupted. "I called them already and they referred me to you."

I paused. "How old is your grandson?"

"Three," he blurted.

"I'm sorry, Mr. Ashly. Children can't fly as unescorted minors if they're under five. Government regulations don't allow it."

I was totally unprepared for what happened next. "I *know* the rules," he began—and then I heard harsh sobs.

I listened in silence, groping for something to say.

He coughed, trying to get hold of himself. "Please, listen to me."

"Certainly, take your time," I said, meaning it. The call was no longer just a nuisance.

In a still unsteady voice, the man explained that his grandson Jody* was about to be placed in a foster home—unless he could be flown to New York to live with his grandparents. The boy's father—Mr. Ashly's son—and mother were drug addicts. They "loved" the child, but couldn't take responsibility for his care.

Something odd began to happen as I listened to this man describe the situation. I was picturing in my mind the small, unwanted boy—the loss, the confusion he must feel, his worry and fear. Gradually the child was no longer Jody, but me, and I was sitting on my father's lap saying, "Daddy, if you say you love me, why don't you stay with me? Why do you want to leave?"

What a rotten situation!

I took a deep breath and spoke into the phone. "Can you fly to Los Angeles yourself to get Jody?"

"Uh . . . no. I—I've had to borrow money just to cover his one-way fare."

Even as I was suggesting other possibilities—and Mr. Ashly was telling me why none of them was feasible for one reason or another

*The name has been changed.

—an idea was rapidly, urgently forming in my mind. And suddenly, instead of thinking about it, I was saying it out loud, as if it were something beyond my control. "Mr. Ashly, tomorrow's my day off and I can fly to Los Angeles and back for next to nothing. I'll pick up Jody for you."

For a moment I thought the line had gone dead, the silence was so complete. Then the words burst from him like the ta-*rah* in a trumpet fanfare. "*You will?*"

"I will. Now give me your phone number and as soon as I find out what flights I can get on I'll call you back and we'll figure out the details."

For a minute or two after hanging up the phone I was very still, thinking about this unknown little boy whose parents were sending him away. It made me angry. I wondered if he would grow up as I had with a hurting place, deep inside, that never seemed to heal. A hurt that was my father's fault . . .

My day was even busier than usual, but with making flight arrangements for Jody and me, it passed quickly. Knowing how tiring the trip would be, I went to bed early, but I did not sleep well. I got up before the alarm went off and at six o'clock, carrying a bag with toy cars, crayons and storybooks, I left my house for Kennedy International Airport.

I'd arranged to meet the Ashlys at the airline's information counter and had given them a description of what I would be wearing. No one was waiting when I arrived. Then I heard a tentative voice behind me. "Miss Vazquez?"

Both Ashlys looked pale and drawn, but when I greeted them, their faces glowed. "Oh, Miss Vazquez, there's no way we can thank you!"

"Please call me Lisa. I'm glad things are working out."

Mr. Ashly gave me a ticket for Jody and told me the boy's father would be bringing him to the airport. He shook my hand wordlessly. Mrs. Ashly hugged me. "I don't know why you're going to so much trouble for us, Lisa, but God's love is surely working through you."

God's love? I wondered about that. God's love was supposed to bring peace, but Mr. Ashly's phone call the previous morning had

stirred up feelings of self-doubt and resentment that I'd struggled with and tried to keep buried nearly all my life. My father was to blame for these feelings. He hadn't loved me enough to stay with me. Way down inside, I believed God didn't love me, either.

My flight departure was announced then. The Ashlys walked me to the security checkpoint. "Tonight Jody and I will meet you right here," I assured them, and hurried off to the boarding gate.

On the plane, with a row of seats to myself, I leaned back and closed my eyes, wishing I could close off my troubling thoughts as easily. . . . My mother, like Mrs. Ashly, believed in God's love. She'd gone on trusting Him even when my father abandoned her. That had happened not long after we'd moved from Puerto Rico to New York. She was in a city foreign to her, where people spoke a language she didn't understand. She had three small children—I was four and my two sisters were only a few years older—and she had no money. Yet her faith never wavered. It was expressed in three words I heard her use over and over again. "God will provide."

And I had to admit that He *did* provide, through His good people. When we arrived in New York City we began to attend a small church and developed close ties with the parishioners. After my father left, they became like a second family to us. One couple in particular saw us through the most needy and difficult times.

Over my lifetime, I'd often seen God working through others. I just didn't believe I mattered to Him.

As the plane drew nearer to Los Angeles, I began to fidget and worry. Even though the Ashlys had talked to Jody on the phone about traveling with me, I wondered how this little boy would react to leaving his parents and coming to New York with a total stranger. What if he cried and clung to his father? What if he refused to leave? Could I handle a wrenching emotional scene? Jody was sure to be confused and frightened. It all seemed so hopeless.

I turned and looked out the small window. The high altitude

created a mystical world of towering cloud formations reaching to who knew what. _Are You out there, God?_ The words came into my mind slowly, as if part of me were resisting them. _Please. I'm not asking for me. Just please be with this little boy and help him . . ._

Jody and I were due to board a return flight to New York less than forty-five minutes after my arrival, so I arranged with a stewardess to sit near the door as we landed to be able to get off quickly. In the terminal, I scanned the clusters of people waiting in the arrival area, looking for a child like the one in the snapshot the Ashlys had given me. Near the exit, I saw a small boy hanging over the railing. Instinctively, I walked up to him and ruffled his hair. "Are you Jody?"

He looked up at me with the most beautiful sky-blue eyes I'd ever seen and smiled hesitantly. "Wee-sa?"

The man standing next to him was unkempt and glassy-eyed. "You're Miss Vazquez?" he said in a monotone. Clearly he was on some kind of drug trip.

"Yes." I glanced at the suitcase he was holding. "Look, our time is short. I'll take the case and check it through and find out the gate number. Wait here."

I dashed down the corridor to the baggage check-in, got a tag for the suitcase and studied the departure board. Hurrying back, I could see that Jody's father had become restless. He was pacing back and forth, twisting his head to look for me. Jody stood forlornly, a wet streak glistening on his cheek.

O God, please.

I rushed up to Jody and knelt beside him. "Hey, what's the matter, guy?" I said, forcing a cheerful voice. "You ought to be practicing your smile for Grandma and Grandpa."

"Oh, Wee-sa, I thought you weft me." And then his soft little arms went around me.

My breath caught. I pulled him close, so close I could feel his heartbeat. Our warmth mingled. God had answered my prayer! I felt an astonishing lightness. Not only relief that Jody trusted me, but as if I had let go of a weight I'd been dragging around with me for a long time. With his simplicity of heart, Jody had shown me the way: Don't hang on to hurt. Let it go and reach for love.

Isn't that what I should have done with the hurt my father caused me? By focusing on the fault—blaming my father, myself, even God—I had kept the wound open. I had not allowed God's love to heal my emotional pain.

I squeezed Jody hard. "No sirree, I won't leave you. You're stuck with me all the way to New York."

I stood up briskly and turned to Jody's father. He was on edge, distracted. I looked at him calmly. He was young, probably younger than I was. Like my father, he had no idea what he was doing—to himself and to others. Maybe some day he would understand and forgive himself. And be forgiven.

"Jody," I said gently, "give your daddy a good-bye kiss."

A moment later, hand-in-hand, we headed for the gate. On the plane, Jody soon drifted off to sleep in the curve of my arm, his upturned face relaxed and trusting, a reflection of my own. It was a good way to travel. The best.

"Thank You, Father," I whispered.

*B*ILLY'S FRIEND

Karen Gasperino

The six of us—my husband, Joey, and I and our four kids—left the house in such a flurry that August day in 1980 that I forgot to put a slip on. *Never mind, Karen,* I told myself. *Considering your state of excitement, it's a wonder your shoes even match!* Only a few hours earlier we'd had a phone call from Mother Teresa, who had recently visited the Pope and President Carter. She wanted to see our family during her brief stay at the Missionaries of Charity convent in the Bronx, New York City's northern borough, just a short drive from our upstate village.

The reason for the invitation was Billy, our three-year-old son from India. This cinnamon-skinned little boy, born without arms, had become a particular favorite of Mother Teresa's after he was brought to the Missionaries of Charity in Calcutta, and she had personally taken him on the train to Delhi when he was sponsored for adoption.

Now the two would see each other for the first time in a year. We were thrilled that the rest of our children were invited too: Mario, nine, our biological son; Stephen, six, our Korea-born son; and Amy, five, our dark-eyed daughter from India.

As we drove in our red station wagon toward New York, I thought about our family. We're ordinary people living in a small, quiet town with five churches. We're not sophisticated. Not people you might expect to have an "international" family. But that's the way it worked out. Joey started it all after he saw a television program about children orphaned by an earthquake in South America. Something about those children touched him. "What about adopting a child whose parents are gone?" he said to me.

My eyes widened. I'd never given a serious thought to adopting. But now I felt a humming inside, a little signal that this was right for us, especially the idea of a child from another culture. So we started the paperwork, and after the usual complications and delays, Stephen came into our lives. We loved him so much that he led to our adopting Amy; and after enjoying our new little girl for a while, Joey and I were saying to each other, "It's time for another."

We called Kathy Shreedhar, who'd helped us with the arrangements for Stephen and Amy, and this time she asked, "What about a child with a handicap?"

"I don't think so," was my reaction.

But Joey's reaction was, "And who do you think is gonna take those kids?"

I fought it, but Joey kept at it until I agreed that we could "just consider" descriptive material about specific handicapped children who were up for adoption. Joey was the first to read the mail the day the material came. "Take a look at these kids!" he said brightly. Innocently. "See if you can tell which one I like."

So we're "just considering," eh? I began to riffle noisily through the pages. Then I stopped, staring at an eager, impish, hey-look-me-over little face. No arms? No matter. I drew a breath. "Billy's my choice," I said.

Joey nodded. "Mine too."

Now we can't imagine life without him.

At the convent, we were led to a small, immaculately clean room with fresh white paint on the walls and a few straight wooden chairs. In its pristine simplicity, it seemed the perfect place to meet Mother Teresa. As we waited, we could hear her laughing and talking warmly in the next room, where she was having tea with the sisters.

Soon a movement at the curtains in the doorway caught our attention. An alert brown face appeared, eyes sparkling, framed in a white headcloth with blue borders; it vanished and appeared again. Mother Teresa was playing peekaboo with the little ones. Then she came into the room, bringing an air of vitality that lent tallness to her small, slender frame. Her face shone as she smiled at the four children. But it was Billy with his empty sleeves who drew from her the tenderest look I have ever seen. As they gazed at each other, a dazzling grin burst through his solemn expression, puffing out his little cheeks, and he leaned his head against her shoulder.

As Mother Teresa, ever the teacher, chatted with the children about school and the homey details of their daily lives, her hand would steal out and stroke Billy's wavy brown hair. She'd cock her head, taking him in, assessing him. "He looks so *well*," she told us again and again.

While I watched this scene, something kept drawing my eye to the floor, nudging for my attention. At last I realized what it was. Beneath her frayed sari, Mother Teresa's feet were bare. And I found them beautiful. Seventy-year-old feet, yet firmly planted. Worn feet, but as sturdy as oak trees. Feet strong enough to have journeyed through seven decades giving care and comfort. Servant's feet that hurried or stood by, depending on the need. Suddenly I wanted to kneel and kiss those faithful feet. But Mother Teresa didn't give me the chance, for the children had her full attention. I watched her as she looked from Billy to Mario to Amy to Stephen and then back to Billy again. "God's children," I heard her say softly, almost to herself. And then she turned to Joey and me. "Thank you," she said.

And all I could think of at that moment was Jesus washing the feet of His disciples. Now, through this tiny, humble woman standing before me, Jesus was washing mine.

ℐ𝒪 QUEST FOR ANGELS

Kimberly Love

Angels have always intrigued me. Just the thought of coming in contact with a real angel sends my imagination soaring. I picture a floating image of beauty and serenity. A soul of perfection casting an aura of peace, with arms extended open to catch the weary; wings designed to embrace and then soar to all corners of the universe in a blink of God's eye. Angels . . . His appointed helpers, His right hand, invisible to the living. Or are they?

When I was twenty, I heard a distant relative say that at the moment her father died, angels came and took him. My father and I listened with intensity to her story as we stood by the coffin while attending her father's wake. When death finally robbed him of his last breath on earth, she said, she beheld a serenity on his face she had never seen. It was as if angels had come and lifted him from his hospital bed before her very eyes.

At that moment, all I could do was exchange an awestruck glance with my dad. Without words, we both knew that what we had just heard wasn't coming from someone with wild delusions. This was an influential scholar, a mother of two children! If she testified that angels came and took her father's soul to heaven, then most likely they did!

At twenty, I had never seen a human being die—but after hearing this story, I almost wanted to! I was determined that someday I, too, would see angels on earth.

During the next eleven years I married, moved to several different states with my husband and had a beautiful daughter. I was no longer a wide-eyed young girl, but an overworked mommy whose brain was clouded with work schedules, demands, mortgage approval and a myriad of worries. Like most young mothers in the 80s, I wanted so much for myself and my family and worked feverishly to have it all. Angels hadn't crossed my mind for quite some time. About the time my stress level peaked at an all time high, I learned my dear father was diagnosed with inoperable pancreatic cancer that had already spread to his liver. He didn't know it then, but he would live only another four weeks.

Inoperable! My grief was overwhelming. Every problem I had ever had paled to this news. I could not imagine the loss of this wonderful man; my mentor, my confidante. This silent, gentle giant of a man whose brain housed the best sense of humor in the world. Cancer was robbing my father's body and fear was robbing my father's soul—he simply couldn't muster even the slightest smile after hearing his diagnosis.

To our rescue came Hospice. After a little time at home, Dad was admitted to one of the Hospice "suites" in Lakeland Hospital in Elkhorn, Wisconsin. Attached to his hospital room was our "apartment." Here our family could sleep, eat, read, watch television, converse freely and still be available to Dad at any moment. Relatives and friends came daily to offer their love and support. Best of all, my parents celebrated their last wedding anniversary surrounded by family and friends in that suite. Everyone sang and ate cake as Dad lay silently in a world of pain. He managed to make it through that day—he didn't want to die on the date he was married.

The following day brought agony and suffering only morphine could dull. Dad was quickly slipping away and the thought of angels haunted me. I needed to walk with my husband. I needed to go outside. As we walked, I shared with him the story I had heard long ago—the angel story. Would the Heavenly Host usher my father from his death bed to everlasting life above the clouds? Would we be there to witness the glory of it? Fortunately, Glenn didn't laugh, nor did he think I was crazy. We simply pondered these things together as we walked.

Evening came and my mother was weary and glassy-eyed. My sister, her husband and their young children needed some different scenery and a decent meal. In his new role as patriarch, my only brother suggested the family go home and get some much needed rest.

My husband and I couldn't go; nor had we any intention of leaving. I was determined to witness the angels. I wanted to be there when Dad's face took on sublime serenity. He deserved it! He had suffered so all day, and if he was to pass away soon, a part of me—my youth—would accompany him. We stayed and promised to phone in the case of an emergency.

Except for the gentle sound of rain drops hitting the window pane, and Dad's deep, laboring breaths, the room was silent now. I watched, broken-hearted, as this shell of the once strong man I cherished struggled to stay in this world. Dad's face was ashen gray, his eyes weren't fully shut or focused and his appearance was a frightening sight.

A hospice nurse entered and offered us some welcome advice. She suggested that because hearing was the last sense to go that we should talk to my father; and so we did—shouting. We proceeded to tell him what we wanted him to remember. We thanked him for our wedding—he'd signed our guest book "Dad Broke Olson"!—for college; for life as we knew it with him; for all his bad jokes. We shouted our thanks in his ear. He heard us, I know. When we had no more to say, for some reason I told him to let go; I wanted to assure him it was okay. He would have done the same for me. Several minutes of silence later, Dad gulped his last breath.

Death did not leave my father looking as though he'd seen the Heavenly Host. He looked as though he'd been lynched by the Grim Reaper. I was horrified. Inside I screamed, *So this is death? How could I be so foolish to believe in angels? God, where are they for this man who served You faithfully all of his life?* My husband and I wept openly. Even a young Hospice nurse couldn't hold back her tears.

For some reason, I suddenly snapped back to the reality of this situation and realized my family needed to be called. They would want to return to the hospital. I turned to Glenn and said, "Help me. Mom can't see Dad like this." Together we gently shut my Father's eyes and closed his open jaw. I fixed his hair and bed, and with the help of the nurses, we propped him up and folded his hands. Dad looked serene now—at peace.

We watched from the door to Dad's room as my family came off the elevator and walked hand in hand toward us. Like a host and hostess, Glenn and I led them to Dad's bedside. My mother, dazed and sad, smiled tenderly and said, "He looks so dignified." The whole family concurred.

I exchanged an awestruck glance with my husband, much as I had done years ago in a funeral parlor with my father. We knew without words we had done our job well. We weren't exactly the celestial beings I had always envisioned, but I do know we were God's appointed helpers that night. We had been chosen long ago to rise above what we witnessed. We were given the rare opportunity to say good-bye and thanks together, the strength to hold each other up and the good fortune to help my father cross the threshold to eternal life. Our load was heavy, but with God's help, it was made light, for all concerned.

We saw angels that night—ourselves.

*S*ERVICE

There are strange ways of serving God;
You sweep a room or turn a sod,
And suddenly, to your surprise,
You hear the whirr of seraphim,
And find you're under God's own eyes
And building palaces for Him.

—Herman Hagedorn

ANGELS OVER THE ATLANTIC

James A. Sills

September 8, 1984. All day long, angry gray combers have thundered onto the beach adjoining Patrick Air Force Base on Florida's east coast. We watch them from our operations center of a small helicopter detachment of the 39th Aerospace Rescue and Recovery Wing. The waves are spawned by tropical storm Diana, which is swelling to ominous proportions out in the Atlantic.

As we stow our helicopters into the wind-shaken hangars, I hope we won't be called out into the coming storm. *But then, that's what we're here for,* I reason, thinking of our unit's shoulder patch: an angel with white wings encircling the earth. A nice sentiment. In reality it would be an airman in a flight suit and combat boots who would be putting his life on the line.

Will our "angels" be called out tonight? I wonder as the building shudders in the intensifying gale.

My answer soon comes: A sergeant, leaning into the wind, hurries up with a message flapping in his hand. It's a distress call relayed from the Air Force Rescue Coordination Center at Scott Air Force Base near St. Louis. They got it from the U.S. Coast Guard Rescue Center in Miami, whose radio picked it up from a Russian oceanographic ship, the *Akademik Kurchatov,* steaming one hundred ten miles east of us out in the Atlantic. Their doctor appears to have acute appendicitis. Can we get him to a hospital?

Russian! The word catches in my throat. How many times on helicopter surveillance have I had to chase Soviet snoop ships away from Cape Canaveral rocket launchings. Somehow they always seem to show up just when a space shot is planned.

Now one of them is in trouble.

Yet I know that the motto on our shoulder patch, *That Others*

May Live, doesn't specify ideology or nationality. We have to get that Russian to a hospital.

I quickly review procedure: Fly a helicopter out to his ship, hover while lowering a "PJ" (parajumper) on a cable, retrieve both men and fly the doctor to a hospital. In calm weather it's risky. But in a full-blown tropical storm . . . ?

I wince as I think of our "Jolly Green Giant" helicopter, safe in the hangar. Its worn cable hoist will sometimes plummet loose without warning. Most of our mustard-green helicopters are Vietnam survivors; some still have bullet holes.

Ah, but the answer is at hand. Out on our ramp perches a visiting rescue-ready blue-and-white Navy CH-46 with a good hoist. Its twin engines are warmed up, and the pilot says he's ready to go.

Our two PJs, Sgt. Craig Kennedy and Staff Sgt. Mike McFadden, climb into the Navy copter, and with a roar it disappears into the leaden scud.

I'm relieved that help is on the way to the stricken Russian doctor, but soon a sergeant reports: "Captain, the Navy copter radioed that they lost rotor synchronization. They just can't buck the gale."

For a long moment I stare out into the storm, then turn and yell to our crew, "The Navy bird's broke! We have to launch!" The lumbering Jolly Green Giant, big rotor blades quivering in the wind, is towed out of the hangar.

The returning Navy copter settles on the ramp; our two PJs leap from it and race to our ship. With flight engineer Bob Rice at the hoist and copilot Capt. Dave Wetlesen at my side, we crank up the Jolly Green, and at 6:50 P.M. we take off.

Our bird yaws and slews in the gale as we head out to sea. We navigate by dead reckoning (if you don't reckon right, you're dead), but somewhere high above the Soviet vessel a Coast Guard radar-equipped Falcon jet is circling. Through our radio, it will guide us in to the Russian ship with vector compass headings.

We chop into the deepening gloom as winds bounce us like a dog shaking a bone. Crew members grip stanchions and I fight to keep on course, my right hand gripping the cyclic that controls lateral movement, my left on the collective which lifts or lowers us, feet working the tail-rotor pedals. It's like trying to dribble four basketballs at once. Below the rain-lashed Plexiglas, huge foam-crested black waves claw at us.

How can we lower a man to a deck that's lunging like a berserk elevator?

I shake my head, kicking right rudder to thrust us back onto vector heading.

Suddenly the Plexiglas blotches over. The windshield wipers have stopped working!

What else can go wrong? Will that worn hoist clutch hold?

I know Dave Wetlesen beside me is praying. He's that kind of guy. As for me, I'm counting on my years of training and rescue experience.

More than an hour passes while the crackling radio feeds us vector headings. Through the streaming Plexiglas I see the glimmer of lights ahead: the Russian ship. As we approach I'm alarmed by its forest of masts and cranes wildly slashing back and forth in the rolling seas.

It'll be like lowering a man into a giant food chopper.

Then we spot a small twenty-foot square deck amidships. Several Soviet sailors wave from it. That's our target.

The 350-foot *Akademik Kurchatov* steams at 15 knots. We radio its captain to head into the wind and slow down.

The vessel swings into the wind but doesn't slow. Evidently their interpreter isn't that good. I grimace, trying to keep our bucking copter even with the moving ship. Directly over it I lose sight of the vessel and also depth perception. Airman Rice leans out the main door calling out directions to guide me.

"Watch her big crane, Captain. It sticks up over one hundred feet."

One hundred feet? My neck hair bristles. Our hoist cable is only 135 feet long. I can almost feel that crane slashing through the aluminum skin of the helicopter's belly.

PJ McFadden, in cable harness, poises at the door.

"Cleared out!" I call. He disappears into the blackness below. Rice carefully works the hoist's worn clutch while directing me: "Right twenty feet . . . steady . . . right some more . . . okay, *hold her!*"

My hands and feet instinctively manipulate the controls to keep us over the target.

Let him miss those masts.

"One hundred feet . . . one-twenty . . . one-thirty . . ." calls out Rice as he pays out almost the last bit of cable. McFadden should soon reach the deck.

"Oh, my God!" exclaims Rice. "Stop forward!"

"What happened?" I choke as I pull back on the cyclic, easing our forward movement.

"The ship suddenly slowed, Captain, and we overshot. McFadden tangled in an antenna, then slammed into the super-structure."

I feel sick. Smashing into the steel wall could shatter every bone in his body.

"How is he? Can you see?"

Rice peers into the dark. Then he exhales in relief. "McFadden's okay, Captain. He picked himself up. He's giving us a thumbs-up!"

Thank You, Lord.

The copter rears like a mad bronco as I fight to hold it above the ship's gyrating masts and cranes. Down on its deck the doctor, hunched in pain, hobbles to our PJ, who buckles them both into the harness and signals us to hoist.

The winch groans, and I find myself praying for that clutch until the two dripping men are hauled aboard.

Now we must fly one hundred fifty miles to the Titusville, Florida, hospital, Fighting the winds of the tropical storm, we struggle along at a ground speed of only fifty miles per hour. We're getting low on fuel. Thank God the Falcon jet is still up there, an angel, really. Flying big figure eights above our slow-moving ship, he guides us through the weather, around dangerous thunderheads.

Drained, I turned over the controls to copilot Wetlesen and slump back. Now, all we have to do is—

Boom! A blinding blue-white flash explodes around us. Lightning!

I chill. Lightning loves airplanes and helicopters. What else can happen?

Another bolt shakes us. Will I ever see my wife, Sindi, and ten-year-old daughter, Christine, again?

Then I remember Alaska, my previous station: six years of almost daily rescues we shouldn't have survived. Once, a fog-hidden mountainside, just yards away, suddenly loomed in our windshield. We missed it by careening the helicopter on its side. Then there was the blizzard-shrouded granite cliff that later we learned our ice-laden ship had cleared by inches. Something, *Someone*, had pulled us through. A peace comes over me and I find myself relaxing, the copter's roar subsiding. *Maybe*, I think, *maybe when people work hard to help others, God gives them that extra edge to see them through.*

Wasn't our motto, *That Others May Live*, another way of saying: "Greater love hath no man than this, that a man lay down his life for his friends" (John 15:13)?

Thinking of that shoulder patch, I find myself smiling. Maybe when we face the impossible, He gives us angels too, real ones, something like that Falcon jet flying invisibly above us, guiding us to safety.

"Lights, Captain!"

It's Melbourne, Florida. The coast.

Soon we settle onto the rain-slick asphalt of the Titusville hospital helipad; medics hurry the Russian doctor into the emergency entrance. It's 9:10 P.M. As I stand by our faithful Jolly Green, I look up and pat its wet flank affectionately.

Then one of my men rushes up. Now what?

"Captain, seems we're in trouble. The State Department says they haven't cleared the Russian into the country yet."

I look at him and he stares back. Then we both look up into Diana's rainy face and laugh.

*M*RS. B. AND HER BUTTERMILK BISCUITS

Idella Bodie

The year was 1948. In our bleak apartment—World War II army barracks converted into ex-GI housing—
I paced concrete floors with our infant daughter Susanne. My arms ached. Needlelike pains knotted in my shoulders and shot up my neck.

Through the large plate-glass windows on either end of the all-in-one living-dining-kitchen area, I looked out at a raw wind whipping leaves against the monotonous asphalt sheeting stretching over row after row of flat army-green housing units. Despair blanketed me like the oncoming winter evening.

Barely more than a year ago I had married Jim, an engineering student at the University of South Carolina. We were both twenty years old. Our plans included my working until he got through school, but an early pregnancy had curtailed that. I had always longed for a family, and I thanked God daily for our precious daughter, but I was weary in body, mind and soul. I could feel my zest for life slipping away and I did not have the power to do anything about it.

Jim would be coming in soon from his off-school hours of selling shoes—a job he'd taken to supplement our $90-a-month income from the GI Bill. We would have our usual end-of-the-month dinner of grilled cheese sandwiches and apple sauce before he hunched over his grueling academic studies.

At age twenty-one we were broke (the birth of our baby had drained our meager savings) and bone tired from wrestling with a colicky daughter until wee morning hours.

I had tried feeding our infant more often, feeding her fewer times, placing a warm water bottle on her little tummy, and every other bit of advice to calm the balled-fists screams and painful squirming. But nothing worked except holding her close during the rhythm of walking and patting her supple back. That, however, took energy, and mine was draining away like dingy dishwater slurping from the kitchen sink.

Outside I saw Mrs. B., the manager of the apartments. She plodded against the blustery wind, her shapeless maroon coat billowing out behind her. Wisps of stiff gray hair fanned beneath the odd-looking felt hat she always wore.

Instinctively I stepped back from the window so she wouldn't see me. I was in no mood for her bouyant chatter. Everyone knew she had the reputation for "talking the horns off a billy goat."

I moved through our long room toward the back window. In the dim shadows outside I could see black coal spilling from the bins hugging each apartment—coal dug from leftover piles at the old Columbia Army Air Base to be fed to our big cast-iron stoves for warmth and cooking.

"O Lord," I breathed, "where are You? What's to become of us?"

As if in answer to my plea, a knocking at the other end of the room startled me. Still jostling and patting my fretting daughter, I answered the knock.

It was Mrs. B. with a telephone message. "Honey," she said through the door I held ajar with my free hand, "your husband just called. The car broke down and he didn't want you to worry about his lateness."

Oh, no, not again! my mind screamed. And, feeling somewhat ashamed for not inviting Mrs. B. in, I thanked her and closed the door against the chilling gust. I could see Jim shivering along the busy highway as he leaned under the hood of the used '36 Chevrolet. He would try to repair it himself—there was no money for the car.

Poor Jim. What if he couldn't fix it this time? The news was like a dark blanket thrown over the fears already lurking in my mind.

O God, I feel so awful. How are we going to make it? I wanted to crawl in bed, pull the covers over my head, and sleep forever.

With darkness approaching, I pulled on the overhead bulb dangling from the ceiling. I was about to draw the shades, closing us in for another night in our fight for survival, when I caught sight of Mrs. B. at the back door. *What does she want now?*

Within moments she stood in the middle of the kitchen floor and lifted a white cloth doily to reveal a pan of buttery brown biscuits whose crusts snuggled together in neat little rows, fragrant, freshly baked.

I had a habit of crying when I felt down and someone was nice to me, and I felt my mouth begin to quiver. I swallowed, thanked her and glanced aside so as not to let her see the tears coming from the sob crowding my throat.

"Honey," she said in her ringing voice, "the pleasure was all mine. You see, I got to watch those biscuits rise." Then she let out a laugh that came from down deep and crinkled her eyes. "And you know, some days I feel just like that old blob of dough."

I must have looked at her curiously then, for she explained. "Seeing that little miracle, I think about my Lord shaping me into something worthwhile—just like He does my dough, and I just give myself over to Him."

I pulled a chair from under the kitchen table and Mrs. B. slipped off her coat and reached for my squirming bundle. Mute, I handed it over and watched while she dropped into the chair and cuddled our baby to her bosom.

"Yes, sirree," she went on, "if my Lord can take a piece of old flat dough and make golden biscuits out of it, just think what He can do with one of His own beings. I live by Psalm 31:1—'In Thee, O Lord, do I put my trust'!"

Mrs. B. seemed to have the right touch, for our baby was strangely quiet. When Mrs. B. wasn't cooing and lulling with a rocking movement, she talked on. "Just as I have faith that my buttermilk and baking soda are going to make my biscuits rise, I have the knowledge that Christ is going to lift me up when I'm down."

Mrs. B. down? I'd never thought about such a thing. She was always flitting about, seemingly on top of things—unlike melancholy me.

I placed the fragrant biscuits into the warming oven at the top of the stove, stoked the fire and sat down in the other kitchen chair to listen to Mrs. B.'s light-hearted chatter.

A short time later when I watched Mrs. B. slip into her coat and let herself out, I knew my spirits were lifting. I fed our daughter and, feeling her body mold itself into mine in slumber, I eased her into the large carriage we used as a bassinet. Then, with a surge of energy I had not felt in a long, long time, I climbed up to the cabinet where we'd stored the blackberry jelly made last summer from berries gathered along a country road.

When Jim came in, the burden of his troubles etching his face, I had freshened up and set the table with cheese slices, applesauce and blackberry jelly. The light of a candle gave it all the glow of a special occasion. Then I drew Mrs. B.'s beautiful buttermilk biscuits from the warming oven and their aroma filled the room.

With the carriage pulled close and a nudge from my foot to keep it gently rocking, the baby quietly—miraculously—watched the candle's flickering flame.

Seeing Jim's face relax, I knew that the faith that Mrs. B. had passed along to me was contagious. And there in the glow of the candlelight, our little family—father, mother and child—came into a mellow circle of love with God in the center.

In my anguish I had questioned God's presence. I had poured out my heart in my misery, but I had not, as Mrs. B. said, allowed Him to take over my weary body and mold me into something new.

And since then, whenever I'm depressed, I remember Mrs. B. and her buttermilk biscuits. It reminds me to put my trust in the Lord, because I know He is there and will lift me up.

*O*UR SUNDAY VISITOR

Shirley McClintock

Boing . . . boing . . . boing . . . The kitchen clock was chiming seven when I finally heard Ken come through the front door, and I could have boinged *him.* Late for supper again. I shoved a casserole in the oven and fumed while Ken hung up his coat and visited with our sons, Steven and Tim.

I realized that my husband, an attorney with a busy general practice, couldn't usher every client out of his office at precisely five. But he didn't even try! If someone had a problem, he'd let him talk and talk and talk. Sometimes Ken didn't even charge him, despite the fact that we needed the money.

When he strolled into the kitchen a few minutes later and asked, "Is dinner ready?" I exploded.

"No it isn't! Why should it be? I never have any idea when you're coming home!"

"Sorry," he apologized. "I had a late client." He looked around the kitchen, noting the exact stage of meal preparation with legal precision. "Can I help? Set the table or make a salad?"

"Just get out of here and leave me alone!" I ordered.

Bewildered, Ken retreated.

Three minutes later I changed my mind. "Come visit with me!" I demanded. But Ken was reading the newspaper and didn't hear.

Dinner, when we finally ate, was a silent affair. Lately, our marriage resembled an armed truce. The more I pleaded for openness and communication, the more silent and withdrawn Ken became. The more he withdrew, the angrier I got.

"Talk to me!" I'd plead with him. "I want to know what you

think, what you feel!" I left my real plea unspoken: "Love me . . . let me know you truly love me."

All my life I'd longed for the kind of love that would wrap around me and keep me warm. My parents loved me and I'd experienced several revelations of God's love. But I wanted something more—something no one, not even my husband, seemed able to give. Was there some deep, dark secret to being loved? Did only a few chosen people experience it?

Our marriage was at the breaking point, but no one knew it. Not our relatives, not our friends, not our fellow church members. Outwardly we were a good Christian family. We attended church each week. Ken narrated the Easter cantata and I occasionally sang solos. We practiced biblical hospitality—"Cheerfully share your home with those who need a meal" (1 Peter 4:9, TLB).

In fact, that's how Hall Moxley came into our lives. I felt so sorry for the poor man that I invited him home for Sunday dinner.

Ken and I had known Hall slightly for years. Once he'd been a prominent cattleman and successful farmer, but his erratic, unpredictable behavior and poor business decisions had cost him everything. Bit by bit, he'd lost his cattle, his land and even his family.

Eventually doctors discovered his problem: a massive brain tumor with roots reaching deep inside the brain. They'd been able to remove only part of it. Cobalt treatments helped but could only slow the tumor's growth temporarily.

A home-cooked meal wasn't much but it was all I had to offer. Besides, it meant someone to talk to. Ken didn't talk to me anymore. Hall was considered a bit strange by some people, but so what? We could manage for one meal.

To our surprise, having him was fun! His compliments on the roast beef and angel food cake delighted me. "Mmmmmmmmm! This food is so-o-o-o good!" he said over and over. With his elbow he poked Tim, who was gulping his dinner. "Slow down, boy! Take your time and enjoy this delicious meal."

Later Hall told us how God's love had sustained him through every crisis. Not even the doctors' ominous "perhaps only six months to live" shook his abiding faith or his desire to spread God's

love to others. Hall's special concern was for
the sick. He visited the hospital and nursing
home every week.

"Only two things really hurt," he confided.
"Losing my family and not being able to read
the Bible like I used to. Sometimes it takes me
an hour to work through ten verses of Scripture!"

Then he brightened. "But I can still love! And that's the
most important thing there is."

Hall—always wearing the same brown cowboy-cut suit—
became a regular Sunday guest. The boys considered him a best
friend; he romped and played right along with them. He provided
out-of-the-office companionship for Ken. And me? I relished his
openness, not to mention his appreciation of my cooking.
Sometimes his visit was the highlight of my week. One Sunday
when Ken stepped out of the room, I poured out the story of our
troubled marriage. "Ken won't communicate with me!" I wailed.
"He won't give of himself!" I lowered my voice so Steven and Tim
wouldn't hear. "We're considering separation. In fact, Ken's slept at
the office the last few nights."

Hall's forehead wrinkled in distress. "Oh, no, Shirley! You can't
let your family break up! No! No! No!"

Right then and there he bowed his head, folded his rough hands
and prayed for us: "Dear Jesus, please help my good friends Ken
and Shirley and the boys. And please show me how to help them,
too. Amen."

He turned to me. "I'll pray for you every day, Shirley," he
promised.

I thanked him, but I doubted he'd remember. His memory was
so poor! Anyway, I didn't see how such simple, childlike prayers
could help with our complicated problems.

Hall surprised me. He remembered, he prayed, and a couple of
weeks later he told me he'd received an answer. "The Lord showed
me where you and Ken should begin," he insisted.

The minute I'd finished the dinner dishes, Hall made Ken and me
sit down at the kitchen table. He took two sheets of paper from his
pocket, found a couple of pencils and shoved them toward us.

"Shirley," he said sternly, "write down five things you like about Ken." He turned to Ken. "Ken, you write five things you like about Shirley."

Ken and I looked at each other in embarrassment. "Oh, Hall, no! This is ridiculous!"

"Write!" he ordered, folding his arms and glaring at us.

Five things? I couldn't even think of one. I glanced at Ken. His pencil, too, was poised above still-blank paper. Then I noticed his arms—those strong, hairy arms that had attracted me to Ken in the first place. I still liked them, so I wrote: #1. *Strong, hairy arms.*

I thought a while longer. Ken wasn't only strong, he was also gentle: #2. *He's gentle.* And Ken was patient: #3. *He's patient.* Whew! Three down, only two to go. Well . . . Ken was always kind, and he practically never said anything bad about anyone: #4. *He's kind.* #5. *He's rarely critical.*

I assumed Hall was going to pray about our lists. I assumed wrong. "Now you must read your lists to each other," he instructed.

What a revelation! It had been years since I'd *told* Ken how much I liked his arms. He never told me he appreciated my cooking and housekeeping skills. I'd never said, "Thank you, Ken, for being patient and kind." He'd never said, "I like your honesty and perceptiveness."

Suddenly Hall's silly little exercise didn't seem quite so silly.

Over the next few weeks, Hall made us delve into our backgrounds. We discovered that my family had been emotional, even explosive, while Ken's had been reserved. Under Hall's guidance we discussed our expectations of marriage—spiritually, financially and physically. We listed traits and habits we wanted the other person to change. We admitted our own shortcomings to each other. Later, when we sought further counseling, we discovered that Hall's methods had been similar to the ones many professionals use to help couples communicate better. But Hall's ideas had come to him through prayer and the inspiration of the Holy Spirit.

Our marriage improved, but I still felt a nagging sense of emptiness. The secret of real love still eluded me. Jesus knew it. Hall knew it. Would I? Ever?

I didn't have much time to dwell on it, though, because Hall's condition was deteriorating. He'd lived an incredible eight years since the tumor had been discovered. Now it was growing again—rapidly—and nothing could halt it.

Twice, tragic fires consumed Hall's homes and his worldly goods. Eventually he was taken to the nursing home where he had visited patients so many times. His mind was nearly gone, his body so wasted he could barely lift his head from the pillow. Yet he still could love. That was obvious from the glow on his face when someone mentioned Jesus.

Hall died September 13, 1984. His funeral was a celebration of victory. Hall had not only triumphed over incredibly adverse circumstances, but he had touched hundreds of people with God's love. The flower-filled church overflowed with those people—black and white, rich and poor, elderly and young.

As the organ signaled the end of the service, I looked past the casket to Ken. We'd both miss Hall, I knew, yet we were glad his ordeal was over. Now he was at home with the Lord, whole and free. As I thought about that, I smiled through my tears. Ken smiled back.

Slowly, in my mind, something registered. *I smiled . . . Ken smiled back.* I gave . . . Ken responded.

That moment, that simple exchange of smiles, stayed with me. I began to understand what Hall had shown me by his own example. To experience love, I had only to give it. I had wanted to be wrapped in a great sense of Ken's love for me, but I had been too wrapped up in myself to seek that love in positive ways. I thanked God that I could change that. I'd start loving Ken tonight—by cooking his favorite meal. I'd zipper my mouth if he was late coming home to dinner. And maybe tomorrow I could begin his day with a big hug and some words of encouragement.

I took a deep breath. At last I knew the secret of love, and it wasn't a secret at all. It was written in one of my favorite Bible verses: "Beloved, let us love one another: for love is of God" (1 John 4:7).

Hall had said the same thing on his first Sunday visit. "I can still love! And that's the most important thing there is."

CHRISTMAS EVE

The door is on the latch tonight
  The hearth-fire is aglow,
I seem to hear soft passing feet—
  The Christ child in the snow.

My heart is open wide tonight
  For stranger, kith or kin;
I would not bar a single door
  Where love might enter in.

                —Kate Douglas Wiggin